SHEET PAN

5-Ingredient Cookbook

SHEET PAN

5-Ingredient Cookbook

Simple, Nutritious, and Delicious Meals

SARAH ANNE JONES

Photos by Bonnie Matthews

Skyhorse Publishing

Skyhorse Publishing books may be purchased in bulk at special discounts for sales promotion, corporate gifts, fund-raising, or educational purposes. Special editions can also be created to specifications. For details, contact the Special Sales Department, Skyhorse Publishing, 307 West 36th Street, 11th Floor, New York, NY 10018 or info@skyhorsepublishing.com.

Skyhorse® and Skyhorse Publishing® are registered trademarks of Skyhorse Publishing, Inc.®, a Delaware corporation.

Visit our website at www.skyhorsepublishing.com.

10 9 8 7 6 5 4 3 2 1

Library of Congress Cataloging-in-Publication Data

Names: Jones, Sarah, 1978- author. | Matthews, Bonnie, 1963- other.
Title: Sheet pan 5-ingredient cookbook : simple, nutritious, and delicious
    meals / Sarah Anne Jones, photos by Bonnie Matthews.
Description: New York, NY : Skyhorse Publishing, [2021] | Includes index. |
    Summary: "75 one-pan recipes made with just a handful of ingredients"--
    Provided by publisher.
Identifiers: LCCN 2021026655 (print) | LCCN 2021026656 (ebook) | ISBN
    9781510766518 (print) | ISBN 9781510768024 (ebook)
Subjects: LCSH: Cooking (Natural foods) | Quick and easy cooking.
Classification: LCC TX741 .J66 2021 (print) | LCC TX741 (ebook) | DDC
    641.5/637--dc23
LC record available at https://lccn.loc.gov/2021026655
LC ebook record available at https://lccn.loc.gov/2021026656

Cover design by Mumtaz Mustafa
Cover photo by Bonnie Matthews

Print ISBN: 978-1-5107-6651-8
Ebook ISBN: 978-1-5107-6802-4

Printed in China

Contents

Introduction vii

Breakfast 1

Appetizers 15

Poultry 29

Beef and Pork 47

Seafood and Vegetarian 73

Desserts 99

Conversion Charts 110
About the Author 111
Index 113

Introduction

There was a time in my life when I considered attending culinary school. Also, embarrassingly, I would perform cooking shows in my kitchen while making such delicacies as boxed macaroni and cheese, ramen noodles, and bologna sandwiches. I loved pretending to be Yan and Julia Child.

I also grew up cooking with my mother and grandmother, as many of us do, and as I grew into adulthood I started reading cookbooks and trying new things. I started to adapt many of the recipes I grew up with to make them better, based on what I learned from these books and, eventually, from the plethora of cooking shows available on TV. Now that both my grandmother and mother have passed away, cooking those meals, and even sometimes using the same cookware we used to use, makes me feel close to them again. Food truly is a language of love.

These days my professional life doesn't involve me making any food. Culinary school never happened, but I do still very much enjoy cooking and eating good food. What I have learned over the years, and what many chefs would tell you, is that the key to a great recipe is usually in using great ingredients. When you're combining great ingredients with flavors that complement each other, you eliminate the need to use a lot of fillers. That makes the cooking process a lot simpler and healthier.

I also happen to be lucky enough to be the working mother of three young children, so simple meals are often a necessity! At the end of a long work day, or honestly even a Saturday, a complicated meal is just not something I want to tackle. But something that includes only five delicious and healthy ingredients? That, I can handle. Then, throw it all on a sheet pan and into the oven, and how can you lose? Being able to provide an easy *and* healthy meal for my growing kids is very satisfying.

This cookbook includes seventy-five recipes that include only five main ingredients, plus some basic everyday staples you likely already have, like olive oil, butter, and salt and pepper. The cookbook includes breakfast, appetizer, dinner, and dessert options that should be able to please all the palates in your family.

WHY SHEET PANS?

In recent years, sheet pans have seen a huge rise in popularity; in a busy, complicated world, it is extremely appealing to limit the amount of prep required and the number of dishes dirtied when making dinner. It's not a new idea, though: it's honestly just the most recent iteration of a thousand-year-old trend towards efficiency.

Sheet pans allow for that all-in-one-dish meal without all the heaviness required in a casserole. For most of these recipes, you can just throw everything onto one pan and forget about it until the timer goes off. On a busy weeknight, time is a priceless commodity.

Another great thing about sheet pan cooking is that everything roasts evenly. Also, because everything is on the same pan, the flavors carry across the entire pan without much effort. When you're using so few ingredients, that allows the harmonies of the flavors to combine perfectly. Roasting also naturally brings out the sugars in many foods, creating that delicious caramelization. Personally, I wasn't a huge fan of vegetables until I started regularly roasting. Now, I can even get my kids to enjoy veggies by roasting them in the oven with some oil, salt, and pepper.

I would also compare the sheet pan to the other "one pan" champions: the electric pressure cooker, or the slow cooker. They do, of course, have their place, and you can't exactly make chili on a sheet pan. But when it comes to chicken and vegetables, or burgers, or pork tenderloin, give me those things roasted any day of the week instead of slow

cooked and broken down into what can sometimes be described as "slop." Vegetables often become unrecognizable after eight hours in a slow cooker. I can't say that's ever been true of a meal I've cooked on my sheet pan. Since picking up the sheet pan habit, my slow cookers and electric pressure cooker have barely seen the outside of their cabinet.

An additional note: unlike your electric appliances, the sheet pan will last you nearly a lifetime, never breaking down on you.

WHICH SHEET PAN?

Sheet pans come in a variety of sizes; the largest size—the full, or 26x18 inch—is most commonly found in commercial kitchens. I doubt the average family needs one quite that large. The one I've used the most often for full dinners is the half size, or 18x13. This is larger than your average cookie sheet. The quarter sheet, which is 13x9, is a great size for crowd-sized desserts. And I really like the eighth sheet, which is 9x6, for family-sized servings of pies and other desserts. It's also great to use if you're just roasting vegetables by themselves.

You can get sheet pans most anywhere you get your kitchen supplies, or you can be like me and order them from Amazon. You can find a great-quality sheet pan for less than $20, and it will likely last you for a really long time. Unlike a lot of our kitchen devices, there's very little you can do to break a sheet pan.

THE 5-INGREDIENT KITCHEN: COMMON PANTRY INGREDIENTS

The focus of this cookbook is that, ultimately, you don't need very many ingredients to create a delicious, quality meal, or appetizer, or dessert. I want you to be able to save time and money with these meals so that you can spend more time with your family and friends.

I approached these recipes with the understanding that most people have some ingredients already in their pantry or refrigerator. To that end, there are some items that will not count toward the five ingredient total of each ingredient, and those are all indicated in italics in the recipe ingredients lists. In addition, some recipes include optional serving ingredients—things like extra toppings for tacos. You can certainly enjoy the recipes without these serving ingredients, but they're listed in case you want to pick them up while you're out shopping.

If you do not have the common pantry ingredients already, stocking them should be both easy and inexpensive. I would recommend making one big shopping trip to pick up some of each of these things to have on hand.

The following basic ingredients are used throughout the book:

Olive Oil:
I use this for nearly all of my meal recipes, especially when they include meat and vegetables. It is a good idea to "splurge" on a good-quality oil, rather than, say, the store brand. I find that the natural flavor in the olive oil is the perfect complement to the flavors in most foods. If you prefer to substitute another oil, feel free to do so.

Salt:
I like salt. A lot. While table salt is perfectly good, I have several different kinds of salt in my pantry, and encourage you to branch out, if you haven't already. You'll start to notice how each salt tastes a little different. I personally prefer coarse sea salt for most of my recipes. But, of course, use whatever you like.

Garlic:
Fresh garlic has the potential to boost flavor in nearly any dish, and carries some well-known health benefits. Adjust the quantities to your preference in any recipe.

Pepper:
Pepper has been an important spice since Roman times. Like salt, there are several varieties, most of which are hugely underutilized in American cuisine. White Pepper is hotter than black, less subtle, and mildly fermented. Green peppercorn is milder in flavor and has a fresher taste.

Citrus:
Lemon, lime, orange, even grapefruit; a small amount of citrus can go a long way in both savory and sweet recipes. I always have, at the very least, those squeeze bottles of both lime and lemon juice in my refrigerator. It also comes in handy when making cocktails.

Onion:
Onion is incredibly versatile and flavorful, and is used around the world as one of the most common basic ingredients. They can also keep for a really long time in your pantry, as long as they are kept cool. Most commonly, I use yellow and red onions, but you can use whatever you prefer.

Sugar:

I'm including both brown and white sugar in this category. I love the richness that brown sugar adds to things like brownies, and of course white, granulated sugar is a must-have in almost any baking recipe.

Vinegar:

Balsamic, apple cider, and white vinegar can be used in pickling liquids, vinaigrettes, and other salad dressings. Vinegar can be an ingredient in many different kinds of sauces and marinades; its high acidity makes it great for helping break down meats, making them more tender. I won't go into the scientific explanation of how vinegar does its thing, but I will say that vinegar has endless uses throughout the home, and that it lasts pretty much forever without being refrigerated. When it comes to balsamic, quality can make a big difference, so you might splurge a little on a good brand of that one.

BREAKFAST

Apple Crumble

PREP TIME: 10 minutes
COOK TIME: 25 minutes
TOTAL TIME: 35 minutes
YIELD: 10–12 servings

This apple crumble is so tart and sweet and perfect for when you want something special for breakfast. Need something to bring to the work breakfast potluck or brunch with friends? Look no further than this recipe.

INGREDIENTS

7 medium apples, Honeycrisp or Jonagold, peeled, cored, and sliced

1 tablespoon lemon juice

1½ cups light brown sugar, packed, divided

1 cup butter, melted, divided

2 teaspoons ground cinnamon, divided

1 pinch coarse salt

2 cups old-fashioned oats

1½ cups all-purpose flour

INSTRUCTIONS

1. Preheat the oven to 425°F. Line a rimmed 13×18-inch sheet pan with parchment paper or coat with nonstick cooking spray.
2. In a large bowl, toss apples with lemon juice, ¼ cup of brown sugar, 2 tablespoons of the melted butter, 1 teaspoon of cinnamon, and a pinch of salt.
3. In another bowl, combine remaining butter, cinnamon, and brown sugar with the oats and flour. Using a fork or your fingers, combine until the mixture resembles coarse sand.
4. Spread the apples on the sheet pan in an even layer. Top with the crumble mixture evenly.
5. Bake for 20–25 minutes, until apples are tender and the top is golden brown.

Junk Food Breakfast, a.k.a. Hangover Savior

PREP TIME: 10 minutes
COOK TIME: 35 minutes
TOTAL TIME: 45 minutes
YIELD: 4 servings

This is similar to what, in New Jersey, they would refer to as "Disco Fries." And if you're getting older, as I am, it may help you harken back nostalgically to those college days of constant hangovers and the need to recover for your 8 a.m. Psych class. Either way, it's delicious and perfect for a weekend breakfast.

INGREDIENTS

1 (2-pound) package crinkle cut french fries

½ cup cheddar cheese

8 slices bacon, uncooked

4 eggs

Salt and pepper, to taste

1 (18-ounce) jar beef gravy, warmed

INSTRUCTIONS

1. Preheat the oven to 400°F. Line a rimmed 13×18-inch sheet pan with parchment paper or coat with nonstick cooking spray.
2. Place the french fries on the sheet pan, and top with cheddar cheese.
3. Bake for 18 minutes. Add bacon slices to the sheet pan and return to the oven for another 7 minutes.
4. Remove the sheet pan from the oven. Make 4 wells on the tray. Carefully crack an egg into each well. Season with salt and pepper.
5. Bake for an additional 10–12 minutes, or until the eggs are set in the middle.
6. Serve topped with gravy.

Egg, Kale, and Bacon Hash

PREP TIME: 10 minutes
COOK TIME: 40–45 minutes
TOTAL TIME: 50–55 minutes
YIELD: 6 servings

(I know kale is one of those things that has become trendy, but the average person won't claim to like it very much. In this recipe, the roasting combined with the bacon makes it absolutely delicious.)

INGREDIENTS

1 pound white or gold potatoes, cut into 2-inch diced pieces

3 cups chopped kale

½ large onion, diced

1 tablespoon olive oil

Coarse salt and pepper to taste

8 slices bacon, cut into 2-inch strips

3 cloves garlic, minced

6 large eggs

¼ cup crumbled goat cheese

INSTRUCTIONS

1. Preheat the oven to 425°F. Line a rimmed 13×18-inch sheet pan with parchment paper or coat with nonstick cooking spray.
2. In a large bowl, toss potatoes, kale, and onion with olive oil, salt, and pepper until coated evenly. Add to the sheet pan in a single layer. Sprinkle bacon pieces evenly over the top.
3. Bake for 20 minutes. Sprinkle with garlic and stir gently.
4. Bake for 15 more minutes or until bacon is crisp and potatoes are fork tender. Remove from the oven.
5. Make six cup-sized spaces on the sheet pan, spaced evenly apart. Crack an egg into each space, being careful to leave the yolks intact. Sprinkle with salt and pepper.
6. Return the pan to the oven and bake for an additional 5–10 minutes or until eggs are set.
7. Remove from the oven. Top with crumbled goat cheese.

Broccoli and Cheddar Slab Quiche

PREP TIME: 15 minutes
COOK TIME: 35 minutes
TOTAL TIME: 50 minutes
YIELD: 10 servings

This dish is amazing to keep on hand for weekly breakfasts or to serve at a brunch with friends! And just like with most of these recipes, the key is using the best possible ingredients—free-range eggs, and good quality broccoli and cheese. You may be inclined to add more seasoning to this dish, but with these ingredients you don't need it.

INGREDIENTS

2 cups broccoli florets

1 sheet puff pastry (thawed, if frozen)

3 large eggs plus 2 large egg yolks

1½ cups whole milk

Salt and pepper, to taste

1½ cups shredded cheddar cheese

INSTRUCTIONS

1. Preheat the oven to 400°F. Line a rimmed 9×13-inch sheet pan with parchment paper or coat with nonstick cooking spray.
2. In a small covered saucepan, bring 1–2 cups of water and the broccoli to a boil. Cook just until crisp-tender, about 4 minutes. Transfer to a colander and rinse with cool water. Chop into small pieces.
3. On a lightly floured surface, roll out the pastry to between $1/8$ and ¼ inch thick. Transfer to the sheet pan, where it should just cover the bottom. Using a fork, prick the bottom all over. Transfer to the refrigerator while you prepare the filling.
4. In a large bowl, or in the bowl of a stand mixer, beat together the eggs and egg yolks. Add the milk, salt, and pepper. Stir in the broccoli and cheddar cheese until well combined.
5. Pour carefully into the prepared sheet pan. Top with a small amount of additional cheese.
6. Bake for 10 minutes. Reduce the oven temperature to 375°F and continue to bake until the filling is set around the edges and bounces back to light pressure in the center, about 25–30 minutes.
7. Serve warm.

Sausage Gravy Breakfast Pizza

PREP TIME: 10 minutes
COOK TIME: 16–20 minutes
TOTAL TIME: 26–30 minutes
YIELD: 8 servings

(This breakfast is definitely a guilty pleasure but will absolutely keep you full for hours. It is also insanely delicious!)

INGREDIENTS

2 cans refrigerated buttermilk biscuits

1 tablespoon olive oil

1 pound uncased breakfast sausage

1 envelope country gravy mix

6 large eggs

1 tablespoon butter

Salt and pepper, to taste

2 cups shredded cheddar cheese

INSTRUCTIONS

1. Preheat the oven to 375°F. Line a rimmed 9×13-inch sheet pan with parchment paper or coat with nonstick cooking spray.
2. Press the biscuit dough into the bottom of the sheet pan, making sure it covers the entire sheet pan and touches the edges.
3. Bake for 11–13 minutes or until golden brown.
4. Meanwhile, in a medium sauté pan, heat olive oil over medium-high heat. Add the sausage, breaking apart with a spatula. Cook until brown throughout. Drain.
5. Prepare the gravy according to package directions. Combine with sausage. Set aside.
6. In a medium bowl, beat the eggs.
7. Melt butter in a large skillet. Add the eggs, salt, and pepper; cook and stir, scrambling until almost set.
8. Top the biscuit crust with the sausage gravy. Layer the eggs over the top, then sprinkle with cheese.
9. Bake for an additional 5–7 minutes or until the cheese is melted.

Blueberry Cinnamon Granola

PREP TIME: 5 minutes
COOK TIME: 20 minutes
TOTAL TIME: 25 minutes
YIELD: 10 servings

(This granola is incredibly versatile—try raisins, raspberries, strawberries. Use honey instead of maple syrup. Add coconut flakes! The options are limitless.)

INGREDIENTS

½ cup olive oil

½ cup maple syrup

½ tablespoon cinnamon

½ teaspoon salt

3 cups old-fashioned rolled oats

1 cup sliced pecans, almonds, or walnuts

1 cup dried blueberries

INSTRUCTIONS

1. Preheat the oven to 300°F. Line a rimmed 13×18-inch sheet pan with parchment paper or coat with nonstick cooking spray.
2. In a medium bowl, combine oil, maple syrup, cinnamon, and salt with a whisk.
3. Add the oats and nuts and toss to coat evenly.
4. Transfer the mixture to the sheet and spread into a single layer.
5. Bake for 20 minutes, stirring halfway through. The granola is done when it is golden brown and the almonds are toasted.
6. Remove the sheet pan from the oven. Sprinkle blueberries over the granola.
7. In order to allow the granola to become clumpy, press it firmly into the pan before it cools. Allow to cool completely before storing.
8. Store in an airtight container in a cool, dry place. The granola can be stored this way for up to one month.

Raspberry Blackberry Sheet Pan Pancakes

PREP TIME: 15 minutes
COOK TIME: 5–15 minutes
TOTAL TIME: 20–30 minutes
YIELD: 12 pancakes

My kids love pancakes. I do not love them, because they are so much work to make and clean up, and they aren't all ready to eat at the same time. These sheet pan pancakes solve both problems. Also, if you have a family of people who likes their pancakes with different fillings, you can switch it up! Make half with the berries, and half with chocolate chips, or nothing at all!

INGREDIENTS

3 cups pancake mix

1½ cups milk

2 large eggs

1½ teaspoons almond extract

1½ cups mix of blackberries and raspberries

Optional serving ingredients: butter, syrup, whipped cream

INSTRUCTIONS

1. Preheat the oven to 425°F. Line a rimmed 13×18-inch sheet pan with parchment paper or coat with nonstick cooking spray.
2. In a large bowl, combine the pancake mix, milk, eggs, and almond extract with a whisk until the batter is smooth.
3. Pour into the sheet pan and spread with spatula until even.
4. Drop the berries onto the batter.
5. Bake for 5–15 minutes or until the pancakes are set and the top is slightly golden brown.
6. Cut into 12 even squares and serve with butter, syrup, and whipped cream.

Sheet Pan French Toast

PREP TIME: 20 minutes
COOK TIME: 8–13 minutes
TOTAL TIME: 28–33 minutes
YIELD: 8 slices

I've had times when I couldn't find brioche in my local store. If you aren't able to, you can use any other sweet, thick-sliced bread. If all else fails, use regular sandwich-thickness bread and reduce the temperature to 400°F.

INGREDIENTS

3 large eggs

½ cup milk

1 teaspoon cinnamon

1 tablespoon white sugar

8 slices brioche

1 tablespoon butter, melted (optional)

Optional serving ingredients: powdered sugar, maple syrup, butter

INSTRUCTIONS

1. Preheat the oven to 450°F. Coat a rimmed 13×18-inch sheet pan with cooking spray or 1 tablespoon melted butter.
2. Once oven is heated, place the empty sheet pan inside for 20 minutes.
3. In a medium bowl, whisk together eggs, milk, cinnamon, and sugar. Put all 8 slices of brioche into the bowl, pushing them into the egg mixture so that all are covered.
4. As soon as the sheet pan is heated, take it out of the oven.
5. Work quickly to place the slices of brioche onto the pan, allowing the excess egg mixture to drip from the bread before placing on the sheet pan.
6. Bake for 5–8 minutes, watching to be sure it doesn't burn.
7. Remove the sheet pan from the oven. Flip the slices and return to the oven to cook for an additional 3–5 minutes, until they are lightly golden brown.
8. Serve topped with powdered sugar, maple syrup, and butter.

Bacon, Zucchini, and Goat Cheese Frittata

PREP TIME: 10 minutes
COOK TIME: 18–25 minutes
TOTAL TIME: 28–35 minutes
YIELD: 6–8 servings

(This dish is perfect for a brunch crowd, or to keep on hand for breakfast throughout the week. It reheats perfectly!)

INGREDIENTS

1 small zucchini

1 tablespoon olive oil

1½ teaspoons salt, divided

1 teaspoon pepper, divided

1 dozen eggs

½ cup half-and-half

8 slices bacon, diced and cooked

4 ounces goat cheese

INSTRUCTIONS

1. Preheat the oven to 375°F. Line a rimmed 13×18-inch sheet pan with parchment paper or coat with nonstick cooking spray.
2. Slice the zucchini lengthwise in half, then into 1-inch half moon shapes. In a small bowl, toss with olive oil, ½ teaspoon salt, and ½ teaspoon pepper.
3. Place in a single layer on the sheet pan. Place in the oven for 5–8 minutes, until just slightly tender.
4. Meanwhile, in a large bowl, beat together eggs, half-and-half, and remaining salt and pepper.
5. Remove sheet pan from oven. Sprinkle bacon evenly over the pan. Carefully pour egg mixture into the sheet pan.
6. Bake for 10–12 minutes, or until eggs have mostly set.
7. Remove from the oven. Crumble goat cheese over the eggs. Bake for an additional 3–5 minutes, or until the top is golden brown.
8. Remove from the oven. Allow to cool 5 minutes before serving.

Sheet Pan Egg-in-a-Hole

PREP TIME: 10 minutes
COOK TIME: 30–34 minutes
TOTAL TIME: 40–44 minutes
YIELD: 6 servings

(I absolutely adore dipping my toast into my egg yolks, but I always find it tricky to time the toast and the eggs and then buttering the toast while it's still warm. By doing it all together on the sheet pan, you eliminate that problem!)

INGREDIENTS

12 breakfast sausage links

6 slices thick bread, such as brioche or Texas toast

3 tablespoons butter, room temperature

6 large eggs

6 ounces cheddar, shredded

Salt and pepper, to taste

INSTRUCTIONS

1. Preheat the oven to 425°F. Line a rimmed 13×18-inch sheet pan with parchment paper or coat with nonstick cooking spray.
2. Place the sausage links on one side of the sheet pan. Bake for 20 minutes, or until they begin to turn golden brown.
3. Using a 3-inch biscuit cutter or a wide-mouth jar, make a hole in each of the slices of bread.
4. Butter one side of each of the slices of bread. Place butter-side down on the sheet pan.
5. Place the sheet pan back in the oven for 2 minutes.
6. Crack one egg into each slice of bread, careful not to break the yolk.
7. Bake for 7–10 minutes, or until egg whites are set.
8. Sprinkle each slice of toast with shredded cheese, and return to the oven for 1–2 minutes, until the cheese is melted.

APPETIZERS

Chicken Wings with Raspberry Glaze

PREP TIME: 10 minutes
COOK TIME: 45–50 minutes
TOTAL TIME: 55–60 minutes
YIELD: 6 servings

(I had some wings similar to these at a wing place in Florida, and was really surprised at how delicious they were. Raspberry and chicken? You have to try it!)

INGREDIENTS

1½–2 pounds chicken wings and drummettes (not frozen)

¼ cup cornstarch or all-purpose flour

Salt and pepper, to taste

¼ cup balsamic vinegar

½ cup seedless raspberry jam

¼ cup hoisin sauce

2 tablespoons butter

INSTRUCTIONS

1. Preheat the oven to 400°F. Line a rimmed 13×18-inch sheet pan with parchment paper or coat with nonstick cooking spray.
2. Pat the chicken wings dry with a towel. In a large bowl, combine the cornstarch or flour, salt, and pepper. Toss the chicken wings in the mixture until they are well-coated. Transfer to the sheet pan, placing them so none of the wings are touching.
3. Bake for 25 minutes. Turn the wings over and bake for another 25–30 minutes or until chicken is golden brown and crispy.
4. In a small saucepan, whisk together the vinegar, jam, and hoisin sauce. Add butter and whisk until melted. Bring to a boil over medium-high heat and allow to boil for 4–5 minutes, whisking constantly, until the sauce is thickened. It should coat the back of a wooden spoon. Allow the sauce to cool.
5. When the chicken is cooked, transfer to a large bowl. Pour the sauce into the bowl and toss until the chicken is coated.

Hasselback Baguette

PREP TIME: 10 minutes
COOK TIME: 15–17 minutes
TOTAL TIME: 35–37 minutes
YIELD: 8–10 servings

(This bread also pairs really well with any kind of Italian dinner with the family, as an alternative to garlic bread.)

INGREDIENTS

1 baguette loaf

1½ cups salted butter

6 cloves garlic, minced

6 sprigs rosemary

8 ounces gorgonzola or feta cheese, crumbled and divided

1 tablespoon coarse salt

INSTRUCTIONS

1. Preheat the oven to 375°F. Line a rimmed 9×13-inch sheet pan with parchment paper or coat with nonstick cooking spray.
2. Place baguette on the sheet pan. Slice into baguette every $1/8$ inch, being careful not to cut all the way through the bread.
3. In a small saucepan, over medium heat, combine butter, garlic, rosemary, 4 ounces cheese, and salt. Cook, stirring intermittently, for 5 minutes, until the butter is melted. Remove from heat. Remove the rosemary sprigs from the mixture.
4. Using a large spoon, pour the butter mixture over the bread, making sure the mixture reaches down into each crevice. Pour any remaining over the top of the bread.
5. Bake for 10–12 minutes, until bread is golden. Top with remaining cheese. Return to the oven and bake for an additional 5 minutes, until the cheese is melted.

Bacon-Wrapped Dates
with Goat Cheese

PREP TIME: 15 minutes

COOK TIME: 15–18 minutes

TOTAL TIME: 30–33 minutes

YIELD: 8 servings (2 dates per person)

I first had this served to me for my birthday several years ago, and I was an instant fan. The sweetness of the dates pairs perfectly with the saltiness of the bacon and the smoothness of the goat cheese.

INGREDIENTS

4 ounces goat cheese

1 tablespoon chipotle powder

16 Medjool dates, pitted

8 slices bacon, cut in half (thin sliced works best)

2 tablespoons brown sugar

INSTRUCTIONS

1. Preheat the oven to 350°F. Line a rimmed 9×13-inch sheet pan with parchment paper or coat with nonstick cooking spray.
2. In a small bowl, mix together the goat cheese and chipotle powder.
3. Using a teaspoon, fill each date with approximately 1^1/$_2$ teaspoons of goat cheese.
4. Wrap each date with a piece of bacon. Place a toothpick through each to hold the bacon in place.
5. Line up the dates on the sheet pan. Sprinkle a small amount of brown sugar on top of each.
6. Bake for 12–15 minutes, until bacon has cooked through. Change the oven temperature to "broil"; leave the sheet pan in the oven for another 2–3 minutes, watching carefully to avoid burning.

Baked Brie

PREP TIME: 10 minutes
COOK TIME: 30 minutes
TOTAL TIME: 40 minutes
YIELD: 8 servings

It is amazing how simple and yet classy this appetizer is. It will impress everyone! You'll be talked about for years (in a good way—not like cousin Sally who always shows up to parties uninvited and drinks all your beer).

INGREDIENTS

1 wheel Brie

1 can refrigerated crescent rolls or 1 large sheet puff pastry

¼ cup seedless blackberry preserves

1 tablespoon butter, melted

1 tablespoon brown sugar

Optional serving ingredients: crackers, apple slices

INSTRUCTIONS

1. Preheat the oven to 350°F. Line a rimmed 9×13-inch sheet pan with parchment paper or coat with nonstick cooking spray.
2. Slice the top rind off the wheel of brie.
3. Lay the crescent roll sheet or pastry flat on the sheet pan. If using crescent roll dough, pinch the seams together.
4. Place the wheel of brie in the center of the dough. Spread the blackberry preserves on top.
5. Fold the dough over the top of the brie, making sure to encase the cheese and preserves. Cut off any excess dough.
6. Brush the top with melted butter. Sprinkle with brown sugar.
7. Bake for 30 minutes, or until golden brown.
8. Allow to cool for 10 minutes. Serve with crackers and apple slices.

Baked Biscuits with Cheesy Spinach Garlic Dip

PREP TIME: 10 minutes
COOK TIME: 30 minutes
TOTAL TIME: 40 minutes
YIELD: 8 servings

(The biggest problem I had with this recipe was that I made it at home when there were just two of us to eat it and we wanted to eat it all!)

INGREDIENTS

1 can refrigerated buttermilk biscuits

2 tablespoons olive oil

1 tablespoon coarse salt

2½ cups shredded mozzarella cheese

²/₃ cup frozen spinach, thawed and chopped

8 ounces cream cheese, room temperature

¹/₃ cup mayonnaise

4 cloves garlic, minced

INSTRUCTIONS

1. Preheat the oven to 350°F. Line a rimmed 6×9-inch sheet pan with parchment paper or coat with nonstick cooking spray.
2. Cut each biscuit in half lengthwise. Roll each half into a ball and place it seam side down around the edge of the sheet pan.
3. Brush the tops of the biscuits with olive oil. Sprinkle with salt.
4. In a medium bowl, combine the remaining ingredients until blended.
5. Pour the dip into the hole created by the biscuits. Smooth the top with a spoon.
6. Bake for 25–30 minutes, until the biscuits are golden brown.

White Pizza Sticks

PREP TIME: 10 minutes
COOK TIME: 10–15 minutes
TOTAL TIME: 20–25 minutes
YIELD: 24 sticks

These sticks are a celebration of cheese. They are also very easy to prepare and will seem a heck of a lot fancier than the effort it required to make them.

INGREDIENTS

1 pound pizza dough, room temperature

2 tablespoons olive oil

4 cloves garlic, pressed or minced

Coarse salt, to taste

2 cups mozzarella cheese

1½ cups ricotta cheese

1 tablespoon dried Italian seasoning

²/₃ cup fresh Parmesan cheese, grated

INSTRUCTIONS

1. Preheat the oven to 450°F. Line a rimmed 13×18-inch sheet pan with parchment paper or coat with nonstick cooking spray.
2. Pull, stretch, and roll out the pizza dough on a lightly floured surface until it is shaped into a rectangle that is approximately 11×17 inches. Carefully transfer to the sheet pan and readjust as necessary once it is on the pan.
3. Brush the dough with the olive oil. Top with garlic, spreading the garlic evenly over the dough. Sprinkle with salt.
4. Top the dough with mozzarella.
5. In a small bowl, combine the ricotta with the dried herbs and salt to taste. Drop by spoonfuls onto the pizza.
6. Top the pizza with the Parmesan.
7. Bake for 10–15 minutes, or until the dough is golden brown and the cheese is melted.
8. Allow to cool for 5 minutes. Cut in half lengthwise and then slice into 2-inch strips horizontally.
9. Serve with marinara sauce, if desired.

Crispy Baked Ravioli

PREP TIME: 10 minutes
COOK TIME: 12–15 minutes
TOTAL TIME: 22–25 minutes
YIELD: 10 servings

(This dish has a delightul crispy outside and a soft, cheesy inside. You can also try alternative dipping sauces, like pesto.)

INGREDIENTS

2 eggs

½ cup seasoned bread crumbs

½ cup grated Parmesan cheese

1 (14-ounce) package cheese ravioli (if frozen, should be thawed)

¼ cup butter, melted

½ cup marinara sauce

INSTRUCTIONS

1. Preheat the oven to 400°F. Line a rimmed 9×13-inch sheet pan with parchment paper or coat with nonstick cooking spray.
2. In one small bowl, beat the eggs. In another bowl, combine the bread crumbs and Parmesan cheese.
3. Dip each ravioli into the eggs, then into the bread crumbs, making sure each is completely coated. Shake off any excess. Transfer to sheet pan, forming lines with the ravioli.
4. Once all ravioli are on the sheet pan, brush each lightly with butter.
5. Bake for 12–15 minutes, or until ravioli are golden brown.
6. Serve with the marinara sauce for dipping.

Sheet Pan Nachos

PREP TIME: 15 minutes
COOK TIME: 5–7 minutes
TOTAL TIME: 20–22 minutes
YIELD: 10 servings

I won't be mad at you if you decide to eat this as dinner and serve with a pitcher of margaritas. These nachos are obviously very flexible: top with tomatoes, cilantro, sliced jalapeños, etc. Whatever you want! I picked what I felt offered the most flavor with just five ingredients.

INGREDIENTS

1 bag tortilla chips

1 (15-ounce) can black beans, drained and rinsed

1 (10-ounce) can sweet corn, drained

Coarse salt, to taste

1½–2 cups shredded Monterey Jack or Mexican cheese blend

½ medium red onion, for garnish

Juice of 1 lime

1 cup salsa, for topping or dipping

Optional serving ingredients: tomatoes, cilantro, sliced jalapeños, sour cream

INSTRUCTIONS

1. Preheat the oven to 400°F. Line a rimmed 13×18-inch sheet pan with parchment paper or coat with nonstick cooking spray.
2. Line the sheet pan with the tortilla chips in a single layer.
3. Top evenly with the black beans and corn. Sprinkle with coarse salt.
4. Top generously with cheese.
5. Bake for 5–7 minutes or until the cheese is melted and bubbly.
6. Remove from the oven and top with onion. Squeeze the lime juice over the pan.
7. Serve with salsa for dipping or top with salsa before serving. Add additional serving ingredients, if desired.

Bacon-Wrapped Sweet Potato Bites with Cheese Dip

PREP TIME: 20 minutes
COOK TIME: 45 minutes
TOTAL TIME: 65 minutes
YIELD: 10 servings of 3 pieces

(I didn't like sweet potatoes for most of my life, but now that I've developed a taste for them, I could probably eat them every day. I love this combinaton with the saltiness of the bacon and the spiciness of the cheese.)

INGREDIENTS

2 large sweet potatoes, peeled and cut into 1-inch cubes

2 tablespoons butter

1 pound bacon, strips cut in half

¼ cup brown sugar

1 tablespoon olive oil

1 medium onion, diced

3 cloves garlic, minced

1 jalapeño, seeded and minced

12 ounces pasteurized American cheese, cubed

½ cup half-and-half

INSTRUCTIONS

1. Preheat the oven to 350°F. Line a rimmed 13×18-inch sheet pan with parchment paper or coat with nonstick cooking spray.
2. In a medium bowl, toss the sweet potatoes with the butter.
3. Wrap each cube of potato with 1 piece of bacon. Secure with a toothpick, and transfer to the sheet pan.
4. Once all the cubes are on the sheet pan, sprinkle with brown sugar.
5. Bake for 40–45 minutes, until the bacon is crisp and the potatoes are tender.
6. While the potatoes are baking: in a small sauté pan over medium-high heat, heat the oil. Add the onions and stir until tender and fragrant, about 5 minutes. Add garlic and jalapeño and sauté until fragrant, about 2 minutes. Remove from heat.
7. In a large, microwave-safe bowl, combine the cheese, half-and-half, and onion mixture.
8. Microwave on high for 2 minutes. Stir and return to the microwave for an additional 3 minutes, stirring at 1-minute intervals until cheese cubes are melted.
9. Remove the potatoes from the oven and serve with cheese dip.

Loaded Waffle Fries

PREP TIME: 5 minutes
COOK TIME: 45 minutes
TOTAL TIME: 50 minutes
YIELD: 6 servings

For this comfort food classic, you can choose to use the salad-aisle bacon pieces, or make your own by frying bacon, allowing it to cool, then breaking it into small pieces.

INGREDIENTS

2 (20-ounce) bags frozen waffle fries
2 cups shredded cheddar cheese
1 cup bacon pieces
½ cup ranch dressing
½ cup chives, minced

INSTRUCTIONS

1. Preheat the oven to 425°F. Line a rimmed 13×18-inch sheet pan with parchment paper or coat with nonstick cooking spray.
2. Place the waffle fries on the sheet pan in a single layer.
3. Bake for 40 minutes.
4. Remove pan from oven. Top with the remaining ingredients.
5. Return to the oven for 3–5 minutes, or until the cheese is melted and bubbling.

POULTRY

Spinach-Stuffed Chicken

PREP TIME: 15 minutes

COOK TIME: 25–30 minutes

TOTAL TIME: 40–45 minutes

YIELD: 4 servings

(I haven't always liked vegetables very much. This recipe, however, is a great way to convince someone to eat their veggies!)

INGREDIENTS

4 boneless, skinless chicken breasts

1 tablespoon olive oil

Salt and pepper, to taste

4 ounces cream cheese, softened

¼ cup grated Parmesan cheese

2 tablespoons mayonnaise

1½ cups fresh spinach, chopped

2 cloves garlic, minced

INSTRUCTIONS

1. Preheat the oven to 375°F. Line a rimmed 13×18-inch sheet pan with parchment paper or coat with nonstick cooking spray.
2. Place the chicken breasts on a cutting board. Drizzle with olive oil; sprinkle with salt and pepper.
3. Using a sharp knife, cut a pocket into the side of each chicken breast. Set aside.
4. In a small bowl, combine cream cheese, Parmesan cheese, mayonnaise, spinach, and garlic.
5. Spoon an equal amount of cream cheese mixture into the chicken breasts. Transfer to the sheet pan.
6. Bake for 25–30 minutes, or until chicken is cooked through.

Barbecue Chicken Dinner

PREP TIME: 10 minutes
COOK TIME: 25 minutes
TOTAL TIME: 35 minutes
YIELD: 4 servings

It's so American, right? The classic summer barbecue dinner. But for many of us, we can't do that year-round. This meal gives you an option to recreate that delicious outdoor meal without cracking open the grill in the middle of winter.

INGREDIENTS

1 pound boneless, skinless chicken breast, cut into tenders

½ cup of barbecue sauce, divided

1 large red onion, chopped

1 large bell pepper, chopped

1 tablespoon olive oil

Salt and pepper, to taste

4 ears of corn, husk and silk removed

2 tablespoons butter

INSTRUCTIONS

1. Preheat the oven to 425°F. Line a rimmed 13×18-inch sheet pan with parchment paper or coat with nonstick cooking spray.
2. In a medium bowl, combine chicken and ¼ cup barbecue sauce. Transfer to the sheet pan.
3. In another medium bowl, combine onion, bell pepper, olive oil, salt, and pepper. Transfer to the sheet pan, leaving space for the corn cobs.
4. Place each cob of corn in a packet of aluminum foil, topping each with ½ tablespoon butter and salt. Add to the sheet pan.
5. Bake for 25 minutes, or until the chicken reaches an internal temperature of 165°F.
6. Brush the chicken with the remaining barbecue sauce.
7. Change the oven setting to "broil". Return the sheet pan to the oven for 2–3 minutes, allowing the barbecue sauce to caramelize.

Herby Turkey and Sweet Potatoes

PREP TIME: 10 minutes
COOK TIME: 40–45 minutes
TOTAL TIME: 50–55 minutes
YIELD: 6 servings

(This recipe is so comforting and tastes just like Thanksgiving dinner. It is so, so much easier though! Serve with cranberry sauce and stuffing and you've got a great meal for chilly days!)

INGREDIENTS

3 tablespoons butter, room temperature

1 teaspoon fresh thyme, minced

1 teaspoon fresh rosemary, minced

½ teaspoon fresh sage, minced

2 cloves garlic, minced

1 teaspoon lemon zest

Coarse salt and black pepper, to taste

1 (2-pound) boneless, skin-on turkey breast

3 medium sweet potatoes

1 tablespoon olive oil

INSTRUCTIONS

1. Preheat the oven to 400°F. Line a rimmed 13×18-inch sheet pan with parchment paper or coat with nonstick cooking spray.
2. In a small bowl, combine butter, herbs, garlic, lemon zest.
3. Place the turkey breast on the sheet pan. With a spoon or your hand, slowly create a space between the skin of the turkey breast and the meat.
4. Spread the butter mixture under the skin, pushing it as far in and as evenly as possible.
5. Generously season the turkey with salt and pepper.
6. Poke the sweet potatoes all over with a fork. Rub with olive oil and sprinkle with salt. Wrap each sweet potato in aluminum foil. Place on the sheet pan.
7. Bake for 40–45 minutes or until the turkey reaches an internal temperature of 160°F and the potatoes are fork tender.

Chicken Drumsticks and Vegetables

PREP TIME: 10 minutes

COOK TIME: 60 minutes

TOTAL TIME: 1 hour, 10 minutes

YIELD: 6 servings

(I think chicken drumsticks are more fun and interesting to eat for kids than chicken breast, with the added benefit of more flavor.)

INGREDIENTS

10 chicken drumsticks

½ cup olive oil, divided

¼ cup brown sugar

1 teaspoon paprika

1 teaspoon salt

1 teaspoon pepper

5 cloves garlic, pressed or minced, divided

2 cups baby carrots

1 medium onion, chopped

2 pounds red potatoes, halved

Salt and pepper, to taste

INSTRUCTIONS

1. Preheat the oven to 375°F. Line a rimmed 13×18-inch sheet pan with parchment paper or coat with nonstick cooking spray.
2. In a large bowl, combine ¼ cup olive oil, brown sugar, paprika, salt, pepper, and 3 cloves garlic. Once combined, add the drumsticks and toss until well coated. Transfer to sheet pan.
3. In a medium bowl, combine remaining olive oil, remaining garlic, baby carrots, onion, potatoes, and salt and pepper to taste. Transfer to the sheet so that everything is in a single layer.
4. Bake for 1 hour, or until drumsticks reach an internal temperature of 160°F and vegetables are fork tender.

Chicken Parmesan

PREP TIME: 10 minutes
COOK TIME: 22 minutes
TOTAL TIME: 32 minutes
YIELD: 6 servings

(Cheesy, saucy, meaty—all the things you love about Italian food, right here! Serve over pasta or, if you're watching your carbs, zucchini noodles.)

INGREDIENTS

1 pound boneless, skinless chicken breasts, pounded to 1-inch thickness

1 egg, beaten

½ cup seasoned bread crumbs

1 cup marinara sauce

1 cup mozzarella cheese, shredded

INSTRUCTIONS

1. Preheat the oven to 375°F. Line a rimmed 13×18-inch sheet pan with parchment paper or coat with nonstick cooking spray.
2. In a medium bowl, beat the eggs. Place the bread crumbs in another medium bowl.
3. Dip each chicken breast into the egg and then into the bread crumbs, making sure to coat chicken well. Transfer chicken to sheet pan.
4. Bake for 10 minutes.
5. Remove from the oven. Spoon tomato sauce onto each chicken breast. Top each with mozzarella.
6. Bake for an additional 10 minutes, or until chicken reaches an internal temperature of 165°F.
7. Turn the oven to broil, and cook for an additional 2 minutes, or until the cheese is golden brown.

Teriyaki Chicken

PREP TIME: 10 minutes
COOK TIME: 20–25 minutes
TOTAL TIME: 30 minutes
YIELD: 4 servings

This recipe is one my mom used to make all the time, particularly on the grill in the summertime. It always tastes like summer to me, and brings back some very fond memories.

INGREDIENTS

¼ cup + 1 tablespoon olive oil, divided

¼ cup soy sauce

6 cloves garlic, crushed or minced

3 tablespoons ketchup

1 tablespoon white vinegar

Salt and pepper, to taste

1½ pounds chicken breasts, pounded to 1-inch thickness

1 bunch asparagus, trimmed

INSTRUCTIONS

1. In a medium bowl, whisk together ¼ cup olive oil, soy sauce, garlic, ketchup, vinegar, salt, and pepper. Add the chicken and cover, marinating 2 hours or up to 24 hours.
2. Preheat the oven to 350°F. Line a rimmed 13×18-inch sheet pan with parchment paper or coat with nonstick cooking spray.
3. Place the asparagus on the sheet pan in a single layer. Drizzle with 1 tablespoon of olive oil. Sprinkle with salt and pepper. Place the chicken on top of the asparagus, also in a single layer.
4. Bake for 20–25 minutes, or until chicken is cooked through.

Honey Mustard Chicken

PREP TIME: 10 minutes
COOK TIME: 30 minutes
TOTAL TIME: 40 minutes
YIELD: 4 servings

(Essentially, you can use any mustard you happen to have on hand for this recipe. I think spicier mustard works better than yellow, though.)

INGREDIENTS

1½ pounds skin-on, boneless chicken thighs

1 tablespoon olive oil

Salt and pepper, to taste

2 tablespoons sour cream

1 tablespoon water

1 tablespoon Dijon mustard

2 teaspoons apple cider vinegar

1 tablespoon honey

INSTRUCTIONS

1. Preheat the oven to 400°F. Line a rimmed 9×13-inch sheet pan with parchment paper or coat with nonstick cooking spray.
2. Place the chicken skin-side down on the sheet pan. Season with salt and pepper.
3. Bake for 15 minutes.
4. Meanwhile, in a small bowl, combine sour cream, water, Dijon mustard, vinegar, and honey.
5. Remove the sheet pan from the oven. Flip the chicken skin-side up. Brush with the sweet mustard sauce.
6. Bake for an additional 15 minutes, or until chicken reaches an internal temperature of 165°F.

Chicken Cordon Bleu

PREP TIME: 10 minutes
COOK TIME: 30 minutes
TOTAL TIME: 40 minutes
YIELD: 4 servings

Chicken Cordon Bleu originated in Paris in the 1840s, and was actually first made with veal, not chicken. It appears to have then appeared in Moscow as Chicken Kiev. It became what we now know as this particular version in the 1940s in America.

INGREDIENTS

4 boneless, skinless chicken breasts

4 ounces deli ham

4 ounces swiss cheese

Salt and pepper, to taste

4 tablespoons olive oil, divided

Creamy Dijon Sauce

½ cup white wine vinegar

2 tablespoons Dijon mustard

2 cloves garlic, minced

2 tablespoons mayonnaise

INSTRUCTIONS

1. Preheat the oven to 350°F. Line a rimmed 13×18-inch sheet pan with parchment paper or coat with nonstick cooking spray.
2. Place the chicken breasts on a cutting board. Cut a pocket into the side of each breast, being careful not to slice all the way through the breast. Place an equal amount of ham and cheese into each breast. Transfer to sheet pan.
3. Drizzle 1 tablespoon olive oil over each breast. Season generously with salt and pepper.
4. Bake for 25–30 minutes, or until chicken is cooked through and juices no longer run clear.
5. While chicken is baking: in a small bowl, combine vinegar, dijon mustard, garlic, and mayonnaise.
6. Remove sheet pan from oven. Pour creamy dijon sauce over the chicken.

Prosciutto-Wrapped Chicken with Kale and Potatoes

PREP TIME: 15 minutes
COOK TIME: 20 minutes
TOTAL TIME: 35 minutes
YIELD: 4 servings

(This meal takes very little time to put together but tastes like you cooked all day!)

INGREDIENTS

2 boneless, skinless chicken breasts

Salt and pepper, to taste

8–12 slices prosciutto

5 tablespoons butter, divided

3 cups potatoes, diced

2 tablespoons olive oil, divided

2 cups kale, chopped

2 cloves garlic, minced

1 tablespoon fresh sage

Juice of 1 lemon

INSTRUCTIONS

1. Preheat the oven to 425°F. Line a rimmed 13×18-inch sheet pan with parchment paper or coat with nonstick cooking spray.
2. Place chicken breasts on a cutting board between 2 pieces of parchment paper. Beat to a 1-inch thickness with a meat mallet or rolling pin. Alternatively, slice in half lengthwise. Sprinkle with salt and pepper.
3. Wrap 2–3 slices of prosciutto around the chicken, so that the breasts are almost completely covered.
4. Place chicken on the sheet pan and drizzle with 2 tablespoons melted butter.
5. In a medium bowl, toss the potatoes with 1 tablespoon olive oil and salt to taste. Spread on the sheet pan in a single layer to one side of the chicken.
6. In a large bowl, toss the kale with 1 tablespoon olive oil, garlic, and sage. Spread on the remaining portion of the sheet pan.
7. Bake for 20 minutes, or until potatoes are fork tender and chicken has reached an internal temperature of 165°F.
8. Whisk together remaining butter, melted, with lemon juice. Drizzle over sheet pan once removed from oven.

Chicken Fajitas

PREP TIME: 10 minutes
COOK TIME: 25 minutes
TOTAL TIME: 45 minutes
YIELD: 6 servings

(These fajitas can be served on tortillas or rice. If you're watching your carbs, there are lower carb tortilla options out there, or you could try cauliflower rice!)

INGREDIENTS

2 tablespoons olive oil

1 packet fajita seasoning

1 pound boneless, skinless chicken breasts, sliced into strips

1 red pepper, sliced

1 green pepper, sliced

1 large onion, sliced

Juice of 1 lime

Optional serving ingredients: tortillas, shredded cheese, cilantro, sour cream

INSTRUCTIONS

1. Preheat the oven to 400°F. Line a 13×18-inch rimmed sheet pan with parchment paper or coat with nonstick cooking spray.
2. In a medium bowl, combine oil and fajita seasoning.
3. Toss chicken and veggies in spice mixture.
4. Spread on sheet pan in a single layer.
5. Bake for 25 minutes or until chicken is cooked through.
6. Remove from the oven. Squeeze juice of lime over the pan. Serve with tortillas, cheese, cilantro, and sour cream.

Parmesan Garlic Chicken with Green Beans

PREP TIME: 15 minutes
COOK TIME: 25 minutes
TOTAL TIME: 40 minutes
YIELD: 4 servings

(This dish is delicious served with rice, pasta, or rolls.)

INGREDIENTS

6 tablespoons olive oil, divided

6 cloves garlic, minced

4 boneless skinless chicken breasts, cut into 2-inch tenderloins

¼ cup grated Parmesan cheese

½ cup panko breadcrumbs

Salt and pepper, to taste

1 pound green beans, trimmed

2 tablespoons butter, melted

½ tablespoon lemon juice

INSTRUCTIONS

1. Preheat the oven to 425°F. Line a 13×18-inch rimmed sheet pan with parchment paper or coat with nonstick cooking spray.
2. Heat 4 tablespoons olive oil and garlic in a small saucepan over medium-low heat, until garlic starts to brown. Transfer to a small bowl.
3. In a medium bowl, combine the Parmesan cheese, panko breadcrumbs, salt, and pepper.
4. Using tongs, dip chicken tenderloins into the garlic-olive oil infusion, then dip into breadcrumb mixture until evenly coated. Transfer to sheet pan.
5. In a medium bowl, toss green beans with remaining olive oil, and salt and pepper. Transfer to the sheet pan and lay in a single layer around the chicken.
6. Bake for 20–25 minutes or until the chicken has reached an internal temperature of 165°F and the green beans are tender.
7. While the sheet pan is in the oven, in a small bowl, combine the butter and lemon juice. Once the sheet pan comes out of the oven, drizzle butter–lemon juice mixture over the chicken and green beans.

Bruschetta Chicken with Balsamic Glaze

PREP TIME: 15 minutes
COOK TIME: 25 minutes
TOTAL TIME: 40 minutes
YIELD: 4 servings

(Very little brings me greater joy than showcasing my homegrown tomatoes in a tasy dish like this Bruschetta Chicken! Even better when you grow your own basil, too!)

INGREDIENTS

Chicken

¼ cup olive oil

3 cloves garlic, minced

1 tablespoon salt

2 teaspoons ground pepper

4 boneless, skinless chicken breasts

Balsamic Glaze

½ cup balsamic vinegar

3 tablespoons brown sugar

Bruschetta Topping

1 pint grape tomatoes, halved

2 tablespoons olive oil

2 tablespoons fresh basil, chopped

5 cloves garlic, minced

Salt and pepper, to taste

INSTRUCTIONS

1. To make the chicken: In a medium-sized bowl, combine the olive oil, garlic, salt, and pepper with a whisk. Add the chicken and cover; marinate for at least 30 minutes, or as long as 12 hours.

2. Preheat the oven to 400°F. Line a 13×18-inch rimmed sheet pan with parchment paper or coat with nonstick cooking spray.

3. Place marinated chicken on the sheet pan. Bake for 20–25 minutes, or until internal temperature reads 165°F.

4. To make the glaze: In a small saucepan over medium heat, combine the balsamic vinegar and brown sugar. Heat to a low boil, whisking occasionally, then reduce heat to medium-low until the vinegar is reduced by half, about 10 minutes. The glaze should coat the back of a spoon when done.

5. Remove from heat and set aside to cool.

6. To make the bruschetta topping: While glaze is cooling, in a small bowl, combine tomatoes, olive oil, basil, garlic, salt, and pepper to taste. Set aside.

7. Spoon bruschetta mixture evenly onto each chicken breast. Top with balsamic glaze.

Pesto Chicken with Tomatoes and Green Beans

PREP TIME: 10 minutes
COOK TIME: 18–22 minutes
TOTAL TIME: 28–32 minutes
YIELD: 4 servings

(Another money-saving and delicious option is to make your own pesto. I've grown my own basil and garlic and just skipped the pine nuts in order to cut costs. I cannot even express how amazing the flavor was!)

INGREDIENTS

1½ pounds boneless, skinless chicken breasts, cut into tenders

½ cup prepared pesto, divided

1 pound green beans, trimmed

Salt and pepper, to taste

1 pint cherry tomatoes

¼ cup fresh shredded Parmesan cheese

Optional serving ingredient: pasta

INSTRUCTIONS

1. Preheat the oven to 400°F. Line a rimmed 9×13-inch sheet pan with parchment paper or coat with nonstick cooking spray.
2. In a medium bowl, combine the chicken with ¼ cup of the pesto until the chicken is coated. Transfer to the sheet pan in a single layer.
3. In another medium bowl, combine the green beans with the remaining pesto. Add to the sheet pan in a single layer.
4. Season chicken and green beans with additional salt and pepper. Bake for 10 minutes.
5. Remove sheet pan from the oven. Add tomatoes in a single layer.
6. Bake for an additional 8–12 minutes or until green beans are tender and chicken is cooked through.
7. Sprinkle with shredded Parmesan and serve with pasta, if desired.

BEEF AND PORK

Barbecue Pork Tenderloin with Green Beans and Tomatoes

PREP TIME: 10 minutes
COOK TIME: 25 minutes
TOTAL TIME: 35 minutes
YIELD: 6 servings

(I think this pairs really well with mashed potatoes, but you could also try rice. I like to have a starch on hand to make sure my growing boys have plenty to keep them full!)

INGREDIENTS

1 (18-ounce) pork tenderloin

¼ cup of your favorite barbecue sauce, divided

1 pound green beans, trimmed

16 ounces cherry tomatoes, halved

2 tablespoons olive oil

Salt and pepper, to taste

INSTRUCTIONS

1. Preheat the oven to 425°F. Line a rimmed 13×18-inch sheet pan with parchment paper or coat with nonstick cooking spray.
2. Place the tenderloin on the sheet pan. Season all over with salt and pepper. Brush one side of the pork with 2 tablespoons of barbecue sauce.
3. Roast for 10 minutes.
4. In a medium bowl, toss green beans and tomatoes with olive oil, salt, and pepper.
5. Remove the sheet pan from the oven. Turn the pork over and brush with remaining barbecue sauce. Add vegetables to the other side of the sheet pan.
6. Return the sheet pan to the oven and bake for 10–15 minutes, or until the pork reaches internal temperature of 145°F and the vegetables are tender.
7. Allow the tenderloin to stand for 10 minutes before slicing.

Kielbasa and Cabbage

PREP TIME: 5 minutes
COOK TIME: 25 minutes
TOTAL TIME: 30 minutes
YIELD: 4 servings

(I love using cabbage to add some crunch to dishes—it really is very versatile and full of nutrition! You could try a combination of green and red cabbage in this recipe.)

INGREDIENTS

3 cloves garlic, minced

2 teaspoons paprika

1 tablespoon olive oil

1 red chili pepper, seeds removed, minced

1 medium green cabbage, sliced thin

1 (12-ounce) package precooked kielbasa or smoked sausage

1 medium red onion, diced

INSTRUCTIONS

1. Preheat the oven to 375°F. Line a rimmed 13×18-inch sheet pan with parchment paper or coat with nonstick cooking spray.
2. In a medium bowl, combine garlic, paprika, 1 tablespoon olive oil, and red chili pepper. Add cabbage and toss to coat.
3. If desired, chop kielbasa into smaller pieces. Place cabbage, kielbasa or sausage, and onion on the sheet pan in a single layer.
4. Bake for 25 minutes.

Ham and Pineapple Dinner

PREP TIME: 5 minutes
COOK TIME: 35 minutes
TOTAL TIME: 40 minutes
YIELD: 4 servings

(Perfect for Easter dinner or, really, any holiday or regular weekend dinner, this meal has the perfect combination of sweet and salty.)

INGREDIENTS

2 large white potatoes, sliced

½ pound baby carrots

2 tablespoons olive oil

2 cloves garlic, minced

Salt and pepper, to taste

½–1 pound ham

½ pineapple, sliced and halved

INSTRUCTIONS

1. Preheat the oven to 350°F. Line a rimmed 13×18-inch sheet pan with parchment paper or coat with nonstick cooking spray.
2. In a medium bowl, toss together the potatoes, carrots, olive oil, garlic, salt, and pepper. Transfer to the sheet pan, placing them on one half to allow room for the ham.
3. Layer ham and pineapple on the other side of the sheet pan.
4. Bake for 35 minutes, stirring potatoes and carrots halfway through.

Stuffed Poblano Peppers

PREP TIME: 15 minutes
COOK TIME: 17 minutes
TOTAL TIME: 55 minutes
YIELD: 4 servings

Prep ground beef in one large batch on the weekend and store in freezer bags. Then it will be ready to go to put these together for your weeknight dinner. You can either thaw overnight or just cook from frozen. Easy peasy lemon squeezy!

INGREDIENTS

4 poblano peppers

1 tablespoon olive oil

1 pound lean ground beef

1 packet taco seasoning

8 ounces cream cheese, softened

1 cup monterey jack or cheddar shredded cheese

INSTRUCTIONS

1. Preheat the oven's broiler. Line a rimmed 13×18-inch sheet pan with parchment paper or coat with nonstick cooking spray.
2. Slice each poblano pepper in half lengthwise. Remove seeds.
3. Place peppers cut-side down on the sheet pan and broil for about 5 minutes, until the skins blister. Remove from the oven and turn open-side up. Set aside.
4. Set the oven to 400°F.
5. Heat a skillet over medium heat. Add olive oil to the pan, then add ground beef and cook until browned. Add taco seasoning and ¼ cup water and reduce over medium heat, about 2 minutes.
6. In a large bowl, combine beef with cream cheese.
7. Stuff each pepper with the beef mixture. Add shredded cheese on top.
8. Bake for 10 minutes, or until the cheese is melted and golden brown.

Zucchini Sausage Pizza Boats

PREP TIME: 15 minutes
COOK TIME: 20 minutes
TOTAL TIME: 35 minutes
YIELD: 4 servings

What is better than saucy, cheesy pizza? Not much, as far as I'm concerned. These zucchini boats will hit that spot, with the added benefits of being a little bit lighter and healthier. You can definitely swap out different toppings if you prefer pepperoni or—God forbid—anchovies.

INGREDIENTS

2 tablespoons olive oil

3 cloves garlic, minced

4–5 medium zucchini, halved lengthwise and flesh scooped out

1 cup marinara or pizza sauce

1 pound spicy Italian sausage, browned

1½ cups shredded mozzarella cheese

Salt and pepper, to taste

INSTRUCTIONS

1. Preheat the oven to 400°F. Line a rimmed 13×18-inch sheet pan with parchment paper or coat with nonstick cooking spray.
2. In a small saucepan, warm olive oil and garlic over medium heat until garlic is just browned. Watch carefully so that the garlic doesn't burn. Remove from heat.
3. Place zucchini on the sheet pan. Brush each with a generous amount of garlic-infused olive oil. Top with equal amounts of sauce, then sausage. Top with equal amounts of cheese.
4. Bake for 18–20 minutes, or until the cheese is melted and golden brown. Add salt and pepper as desired.

Ranch Kielbasa and Zucchini

PREP TIME: 10 minutes
COOK TIME: 15 minutes
TOTAL TIME: 25 minutes
YIELD: 4 servings

 I think goat cheese might be a little "out there" for some people, but I promise it's amazing. If you aren't convinced, you can absolutely skip it for this meal, or substitute with a more preferred cheese.

INGREDIENTS

1 (12-ounce) package precooked kielbasa or smoked sausage, sliced into ½-inch rounds

1 medium/large zucchini, sliced into 1-inch pieces

1 cup cherry tomatoes

1 packet dry ranch seasoning

4 ounces goat cheese

INSTRUCTIONS

1. Preheat the oven to 400°F. Line a rimmed 13×18-inch sheet pan with parchment paper or coat with nonstick cooking spray.
2. In a medium bowl, combine kielbasa, zucchini, and tomatoes. Add the packet of ranch powder and toss to coat.
3. Place kielbasa and vegetables on the sheet pan in a single layer.
4. Bake for 15 minutes or until vegetables are tender.
5. Serve topped with crumbled goat cheese.

Bacon-Wrapped Mini Meat Loaves

PREP TIME: 15 minutes
COOK TIME: 40 minutes
TOTAL TIME: 55 minutes
YIELD: 6 servings

(If you'd like to increase the moisture and/or flavor in this recipe, you can use a mixture of 50/50 ground pork and ground beef.)

INGREDIENTS

1¼ pounds ground beef

½ cup seasoned bread crumbs

1 egg

½ small onion, grated

Salt and pepper, to taste

6 slices bacon

1 tablespoon brown mustard

½ cup brown sugar

INSTRUCTIONS

1. Preheat the oven to 375°F. Line a rimmed 9×13-inch sheet pan with parchment paper or coat with nonstick cooking spray.
2. In a large bowl, combine ground beef, bread crumbs, egg, onion, and salt and pepper.
3. Form the mixture into 6 small loaves, about 2 inches thick. Wrap one slice of bacon around each loaf, tucking the ends under the bottom.
4. In a small bowl, combine mustard and brown sugar. Brush on top of meat loaves.
5. Bake for 40 minutes. Change oven setting to broil and leave in the oven for an additional 2–3 minutes, watching very closely, until the bacon is crisp.

Garlic Herb Pork Tenderloin

PREP TIME: 10 minutes
COOK TIME: 15 minutes
TOTAL TIME: 25 minutes
YIELD: 4 servings

(If you don't have fresh herbs for this dish, you can use dried. I would recommend rubbing the herbs between your hands to release the flavor first.)

INGREDIENTS

1 tablespoon olive oil

1 tablespoon fresh rosemary, minced

2 tablespoons fresh Italian parsley, minced, divided

1 tablespoon fresh basil, minced

Salt and pepper, to taste

4 cloves garlic, minced

1½ pound pork tenderloin

INSTRUCTIONS

1. Preheat the oven to 425°F. Line a rimmed 9×13-inch sheet pan with parchment paper or coat with nonstick cooking spray.
2. In a small bowl, combine olive oil, herbs, salt and pepper, and garlic.
3. Place pork on the sheet pan. Rub with the olive oil/herb mixture.
4. Bake for 15 minutes, or until tenderloin reaches an internal temperature of 145°F.
5. Remove from the oven and allow to rest for 10 minutes. This will help the tenderloin keep its juiciness.

Sheet Pan Tacos

PREP TIME: 5 minutes
COOK TIME: 30 minutes
TOTAL TIME: 35 minutes
YIELD: 8 servings

(Taco Tuesday takes on a different, less-messy form with these sheet pan tacos! Top with all of your taco favorites, and don't worry about dropping them out of the shell!)

INGREDIENTS

2½ pounds lean ground beef

2 packets taco seasoning

2 tablespoons tomato paste

1 cup diced onion

3 cups shredded cheese

Optional serving ingredients: sliced jalapeños, sliced avocado, chopped tomato, salsa, sour cream, cilantro

INSTRUCTIONS

1. Preheat the oven to 400°F. Line a rimmed 9×13-inch sheet pan with parchment paper or coat with nonstick cooking spray.
2. In a large bowl, combine ground beef, taco seasoning, tomato paste, and onion.
3. Spread in the prepared sheet pan. Bake for 20 minutes.
4. Remove pan from oven and top with cheese. Return to the oven for another 10 minutes, or until the cheese is melted.
5. Top as desired with jalapeños, avocado, tomato, salsa, sour cream, or cilantro.

BLT Pizza with Roasted Garlic Aioli

PREP TIME: 10 minutes
COOK TIME: 10–12 minutes
TOTAL TIME: 20–22 minutes
YIELD: 6 servings

(If you don't care for arugula, you can certainly go for the more traditional iceberg or romaine lettuce on this pizza. Arugula has an extra zing to it that I really like!)

INGREDIENTS

1 can refrigerated pizza dough

¼ cup mayonnaise

4 cloves roasted garlic

Salt, to taste

1 cup arugula

6 slices bacon, diced and fried

½ cup cherry tomatoes, halved

INSTRUCTIONS

1. Preheat the oven to 400°F. Line a rimmed 9×13-inch sheet pan with parchment paper or coat with nonstick cooking spray.
2. Press the dough into the sheet pan, stretching it to fill the pan.
3. Bake for 10–12 minutes, or until the dough is golden brown.
4. In a small bowl, stir together the mayonnaise, roasted garlic, and salt.
5. Spread the aioli on the prepared crust. Top with arugula, bacon, and cherry tomatoes.

Roasted Garlic: Prepare a head of garlic by chopping off the top ½ inch. Place on a large piece of aluminum foil, and top with 1 tablespoon of olive oil. Wrap completely in the aluminum foil. Place in the oven for 20–25 minutes. Remove and set aside.

Chili Cheese Pigs in Blankets

PREP TIME: 10 minutes
COOK TIME: 30–40 minutes
TOTAL TIME: 40–50 minutes
YIELD: 4 servings

(This recipe is great for the kids in the family, as well as the kid inside each of us.)

INGREDIENTS

2 cans refrigerated crescent rolls (16 ounces total)

1 package (14 ounces) cocktail weiners

8 ounces shredded cheddar cheese, divided

1 can chili

Red onion, diced

INSTRUCTIONS

1. Preheat the oven to 375°F. Line a rimmed 9×13-inch sheet pan with parchment paper or coat with nonstick cooking spray.
2. Lay out both cans of crescent rolls on a cutting board. Cut each triangle into 3 smaller triangles.
3. Roll each triangle around one sausage and a small sprinkling of cheese. Once rolled, lay in the bottom of the sheet pan.
4. Once all sausages are lining the bottom of the sheet pan, bake for 20–25 minutes, or until the dough is golden brown.
5. Top the sausages with the chili and the remaining cheese. Bake an additional 10–15 minutes, or until the cheese is melted and chili is warmed.
6. Top with red onion.

Pork Tenderloin with Fingerling Potatoes, Apples, and Green Beans

PREP TIME: 10 minutes
COOK TIME: 35 minutes
TOTAL TIME: 45 minutes
YIELD: 6–8 servings

I like to use purple fingerlings with this recipe to add an extra pop of color. However, if you have non-adventurous eaters in your family, perhaps use a mix of purple and white fingerlings.

INGREDIENTS

3 tablespoons olive oil, divided

1½ tablespoons coarse salt, divided

¾ teaspoon pepper, divided

2 tablespoons chopped fresh sage, divided

2 pork tenderloins, 1½ pounds each

1 pound fingerling potatoes, cut into 2-inch pieces

8 ounces green beans, trimmed

1 large onion, chopped

3 cloves garlic, minced

2 large Jonagold or Honeycrisp apples, sliced

INSTRUCTIONS

1. Preheat the oven to 450°F. Line a rimmed 13×18-inch sheet pan with parchment paper or coat with nonstick cooking spray.
2. In a small bowl, combine 1 tablespoon olive oil, ½ tablespoon salt, ¼ teaspoon pepper, and 1 tablespoon sage. Rub on the pork tenderloins. Place in the center of the sheet pan.
3. In a medium bowl, toss the potatoes, green beans, onion, garlic, 2 tablespoons olive oil, 1 tablespoon salt, remaining pepper, and remaining sage. Spread on the sheet pan around the pork.
4. Place sheet pan in oven. Bake for 20 minutes.
5. Add apples to the sheet pan, creating a single layer around the pork as much as possible.
6. Place sheet pan in oven. Bake for 10–15 minutes, or until the internal temperature of the tenderloin reads 150°F and vegetables and apples are cooked to desired tenderness.
7. Allow pork to rest for 10 minutes before serving.

Parmesan Pork Chops

PREP TIME: 10 minutes
COOK TIME: 45 minutes
TOTAL TIME: 55 minutes
YIELD: 4 servings

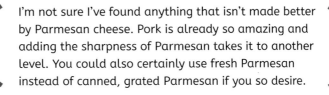

I'm not sure I've found anything that isn't made better by Parmesan cheese. Pork is already so amazing and adding the sharpness of Parmesan takes it to another level. You could also certainly use fresh Parmesan instead of canned, grated Parmesan if you so desire.

INGREDIENTS

1 pound medium red potatoes, halved

3 tablespoons olive oil, divided

Salt and pepper, to taste

½ cup grated Parmesan cheese

½ cup seasoned breadcrumbs

4 boneless pork chops, ½-inch thick

INSTRUCTIONS

1. Preheat the oven to 350°F. Line a 13×18-inch rimmed sheet pan with parchment paper or coat with nonstick cooking spray.
2. In a medium bowl, toss the potatoes together with 1 tablespoon olive oil, salt, and pepper. Transfer to the sheet pan in a single layer, leaving room for the pork chops.
3. In a shallow dish, combine the Parmesan and breadcrumbs.
4. Rub each pork chop all over with olive oil, then dip in the bread crumbs until coated. Transfer each to the sheet pan.
5. Bake for 45 minutes, or until pork reaches internal temperature of 145°F and the potatoes are tender.

Steak Dinner

PREP TIME: 10 minutes
COOK TIME: 25 minutes
TOTAL TIME: 35 minutes
YIELD: 4 servings

(If you prefer your steak cooked well done, you may want to check the potatoes and possibly remove them from the sheet pan before the steak is fully cooked so it can broil on its own. The other option is to place the steak on the sheet pan at the beginning of the baking process.)

INGREDIENTS

3 cloves garlic, minced

1 teaspoon paprika

1 teaspoon dried Italian seasoning

1 teaspoon red pepper flakes

Salt and pepper, to taste

1 tablespoon olive oil

2 cups red potatoes, quartered

1½ pounds New York strip steak

2 tablespoons butter

INSTRUCTIONS

1. Preheat the oven to 425°F. Line a rimmed 13×18-inch sheet pan with parchment paper or coat with nonstick cooking spray.
2. In a medium bowl, combine garlic, paprika, Italian seasoning, red pepper flakes, salt, pepper, and 1 tablespoon olive oil. Add potatoes and toss to coat.
3. Transfer potatoes to the sheet pan in a single layer. Bake for 15 minutes.
4. While the potatoes are baking, place the steak(s) on the counter to allow it to come to room temperature. Season generously with salt and pepper.
5. Remove the sheet pan from the oven. Add steak(s) to the sheet pan, moving potatoes to the side to allow everything to lay in a single layer. Top each steak with a tablespoon of butter.
6. Set the oven to broil.
7. Place the sheet pan back into the oven and broil for 5 minutes. Flip the steak(s); broil for another 5 minutes, or until steaks are to the desired doneness.
8. Remove the sheet pan from the oven. Allow the steaks to rest for 5 minutes before serving.

Philly Cheesesteak

PREP TIME: 5 minutes
COOK TIME: 20 minutes
TOTAL TIME: 25 minutes
YIELD: 4 servings

If you are familiar with the classic Philadelphia sandwich, you know that the type of cheese that should be used is a huge point of contention. Personally, I don't care for American Cheese (call me a cheese snob if you will), but if that's what you like, do it!

INGREDIENTS

1 pound steak (flank, ribeye, sirloin), sliced very thin

1 onion, sliced

2 green bell peppers, sliced

8 ounces mushrooms, sliced

1 tablespoon olive oil

3 cloves garlic, minced

1 teaspoon salt

½ teaspoon pepper

4 slices provolone

Optional serving ingredients: sub rolls

INSTRUCTIONS

1. Preheat the oven to 375°F. Line a rimmed 13×18-inch sheet pan with parchment paper or coat with nonstick cooking spray.
2. Place the steak, vegetables, and garlic on the sheet pan in a single layer. Drizzle with olive oil and season with salt and pepper.
3. Bake for 15 minutes.
4. Remove the sheet pan from the oven. Top with cheese slices and return to the oven. Set the oven to broil and leave in for approximately 5 minutes, until the cheese is melted and golden brown. Watch it carefully so that it doesn't burn.
5. Serve on sub rolls, if desired.

Ranch Sheet Pan Burgers and Fries

PREP TIME: 10 minutes
COOK TIME: 50 minutes
TOTAL TIME: 60 minutes
YIELD: 4 servings

Burgers are one of the few things everyone in my family will eat. I love that this recipe makes it so easy to make burgers for everyone in the family all on one pan with very little mess.

INGREDIENTS

4 medium russet or Yukon gold potatoes

2 tablespoons olive oil

Salt, to taste

1½ pounds ground beef

1 packet dry ranch seasoning

6 slices raw bacon, cut in half

4 slices cheese (optional)

INSTRUCTIONS

1. Peel and wash the potatoes. Cut them into ¼-inch slices. Place them in a large bowl and cover them with hot water. Allow them to soak for at least 30 minutes, but for as much as overnight.
2. Preheat the oven to 400°F. Line a 13×18-inch rimmed sheet pan with parchment paper or coat with nonstick cooking spray.
3. Drain and dry the potatoes thoroughly. It is often easiest to lay them on a paper towel while the oven is heating.
4. In a large bowl, toss the potatoes with the oil and salt. Lay them on the sheet pan in a single layer.
5. Bake for 30 minutes.
6. Meanwhile, combine the ground beef and dry ranch seasoning in a medium bowl. Form into 4 equal patties and set aside.
7. After the potatoes have baked for 30 minutes, remove the sheet pan from the oven. Increase the temperature of the oven to 425°F.
8. Move the fries to one side of the sheet pan, still maintaining a single layer.
9. Get a piece of aluminum foil, slightly larger than half of the sheet pan. Fold up each side, creating a square with small walls, to contain any juice from the burgers. Place on the empty half of the sheet pan.
10. Place the patties on the aluminum foil. Place the bacon around each patty in a single layer.
11. Place the sheet pan back in the oven. Bake for 20 minutes. If using cheese, place on the burgers when they have ~2 minutes remaining.

Steak Tips

PREP TIME: 15 minutes
COOK TIME: 8 minutes
TOTAL TIME: 28 minutes
YIELD: 4 servings

(I recommend tripling this recipe for easy meals later in the week; throw them on top of a salad or throw on a sub roll for a sandwich!)

INGREDIENTS

¼ cup balsamic vinegar

3 cloves garlic, minced

1 tablespoon rosemary, minced

½ teaspoon salt

½ teaspoon black pepper

1 teaspoon Dijon mustard

$1/_3$ cup olive oil

1 pound sirloin steak tips, 1½-inch pieces

INSTRUCTIONS

1. In a medium bowl, whisk together everything except the steak. Reserve half and set aside. Add steak tips and marinate for at least 1 hour or as many as 24 hours.
2. Preheat the oven's broiler. Line a 9×13-inch rimmed sheet pan with parchment paper or coat with nonstick cooking spray.
3. Transfer the steak tips to the sheet pan in a single layer. Place in the oven for 5 minutes.
4. Remove the sheet pan from the oven; flip the steak tips over. Return to the oven for an additional 3 minutes, or until steak tips are to desired doneness.
5. Remove from the oven and allow to rest for 5 minutes. Serve with the reserved marinade.

Beef and Broccoli

PREP TIME: 10 minutes
COOK TIME: 15 minutes
TOTAL TIME: 25 minutes
YIELD: 4 servings

(To make this recipe even easier, you can marinate the beef the night before so it's ready to go when you get home from work.)

INGREDIENTS

½ cup teriyaki sauce (homemade or store bought)

1 tablespoon orange juice

4 *cloves garlic, minced*

1 pound flank steak, cubed

2½ cups broccoli florets

1 *large onion, sliced into rings*

Basmati rice, prepared per instructions on package

INSTRUCTIONS

1. In a medium bowl, combine teriyaki sauce, orange juice, and garlic. Add steak cubes and allow to marinate for 15–30 minutes.
2. Preheat the oven to 425°F. Line a 13×18-inch rimmed sheet pan with parchment paper or coat with nonstick cooking spray.
3. Place steak on the sheet pan in a single layer.
4. Place the broccoli florets in the marinade and toss lightly to coat. Place on the sheet pan with the steak. Add the onion slices.
5. Bake for 12–15 minutes, or until steak is cooked to desired doneness and broccoli is fork-tender.
6. Serve with rice.

Steak Fajitas

PREP TIME: 10 minutes
COOK TIME: 13–18 minutes
TOTAL TIME: 23–28 minutes
YIELD: 6 servings

(This recipe is easily served with tortillas or over rice or salad. It truly works for everyone in the family!)

INGREDIENTS

2 cloves garlic, minced

1 packet fajita seasoning

2 tablespoons olive oil

¼ cup + 1 bunch cilantro, divided

2 tablespoons lime juice

2 pounds flank steak, sliced thin

3 bell peppers, different colors, sliced

2 jalapeño peppers, seeded and sliced

½ red onion, sliced

2 limes, sliced

INSTRUCTIONS

1. Preheat the oven to 425°F. Line a 13×18-inch rimmed sheet pan with parchment paper or coat with nonstick cooking spray.
2. In a large bowl, combine garlic, fajita seasoning, olive oil, ¼ cup cilantro, and lime juice. Add steak, peppers, and onion; stir to combine. Set aside and allow to marinate for 10–15 minutes (or longer if you'd like/are able).
3. Place lime slices in a single layer on the sheet pan.
4. Place the steak and vegetables on the sheet pan, on top of the lime slices, spreading them out as evenly as possible. Bake for 10–15 minutes.
5. Set the oven to broil and leave the sheet pan in the oven for an additional 3 minutes.
6. Remove from the oven and top with more cilantro, if desired.

SEAFOOD AND VEGETARIAN

Mexican Kale and Beans

PREP TIME: 5 minutes
COOK TIME: 15 minutes
TOTAL TIME: 20 minutes
YIELD: 4 servings

(In general, I would say that I am not capable of being a vegetarian full time. But recipes like this one are so satisfying and filling that it might just change my mind!)

INGREDIENTS

4 cups kale, chopped

1½ cups canned Mexican corn blend (corn and peppers)

1 (15-ounce) can black beans, drained and rinsed

1 tablespoon olive oil

1 packet fajita seasoning

Salt and pepper, to taste

¼ cup cotija cheese, crumbled

INSTRUCTIONS

1. Preheat the oven to 400°F. Line a 13×18-inch rimmed sheet pan with parchment paper or coat with nonstick cooking spray.
2. In a large bowl, toss together the kale, corn, beans, olive oil, and fajita seasoning. Transfer to the sheet pan and spread into a single layer. Season with additional salt and pepper.
3. Bake for 15 minutes.
4. Serve topped with crumbled cotija cheese.

Chickpeas and Vegetables

PREP TIME: 15 minutes
COOK TIME: 45 minutes
TOTAL TIME: 1 hour
YIELD: 8 servings

(You can definitely adapt this recipe to whatever vegetables you find at the farmer's market or happen to grow in your garden.)

INGREDIENTS

2 (15-ounce) cans chickpeas, rinsed and drained

½ butternut squash, peeled, sliced, and cut into 1-inch pieces

1 medium onion, diced

1 medium sweet potato, peeled and cut into 1-inch pieces

2 large parsnips, peeled and cut into 1-inch pieces

2 stalks celery, chopped

3 tablespoons olive oil

3 cloves garlic, minced

INSTRUCTIONS

1. Preheat the oven to 350°F. Line a 13×18-inch rimmed sheet pan with parchment paper or coat with nonstick cooking spray.
2. In a large bowl or directly on the sheet pan, toss together all the ingredients, then spread into a single layer.
3. Roast for about 45 minutes, stirring halfway through, or until the vegetables are tender and the chickpeas are slightly crisp.

Gnocchi and Vegetables

PREP TIME: 5 minutes
COOK TIME: 18–20 minutes
TOTAL TIME: 23–25 minutes
YIELD: 4 servings

(The gnocchi in this recipe take on a crispier, toastier texture than you may be used to for gnocchi, kind of like tater tots, but more sophisticated.)

INGREDIENTS

1 package shelf-stable potato gnocchi

½ pound Brussels sprouts, quartered (halved if small)

1 pint grape or cherry tomatoes

1 medium red onion, diced

4 cloves garlic, minced

2 tablespoons basil, chopped

2 tablespoons olive oil

Salt and pepper, to taste

¼ cup fresh grated Parmesan cheese

INSTRUCTIONS

1. Preheat the oven to 450°F. Line a 13x18-inch rimmed sheet pan with parchment paper or coat with nonstick cooking spray.
2. In a large bowl, toss together all ingredients other than the Parmesan. Transfer to the sheet pan, spreading into a single layer.
3. Bake for 18–20 minutes, stirring halfway through, until the vegetables are tender and caramelized.
4. Serve topped with the grated Parmesan cheese.

Quesadilla

PREP TIME: 15 minutes
COOK TIME: 35 minutes
TOTAL TIME: 50 minutes
YIELD: 6 servings

(If you are lucky enough to live in a place with more traditional quesadilla cheeses, I recommend asadero or manchego cheeses for this recipe, split in the quantities below.)

INGREDIENTS

1 tablespoon olive oil

2 bell peppers, chopped or sliced

1 medium onion, chopped or sliced

Salt, to taste

1 (15-ounce) can black beans, drained and rinsed

12 (8-inch) flour tortillas

1 cup Monterey Jack cheese

1 cup mozzarella cheese

Optional serving ingredients: sour cream, salsa

INSTRUCTIONS

1. Preheat the oven to 425°F. Line a 9×13-inch rimmed sheet pan with parchment paper or coat with nonstick cooking spray.
2. In a medium sauté pan, heat the oil over medium heat. Add peppers and onion, seasoning with salt. Cook, stirring occasionally, until soft, about 5 minutes.
3. Transfer veggies to a medium bowl. Add beans and stir to combine.
4. Place 6 tortillas around the edges of the sheet pan, allowing about half of each tortilla to hang over the edges of the pan. Place another tortilla in the center to cover the bottom of the pan completely.
5. Place a layer of cheese on the tortillas, then the veggies and bean filling, then another layer of cheese. Fold over the overhanging tortillas, then place another tortilla over the filling in the center.
6. Place another sheet pan or baking sheet on top of the quesadillas.
7. Bake for 20 minutes. Remove the top baking sheet and return the quesadillas to the oven for 15 minutes, or until the tortillas are lightly golden.
8. Cut into wedges. If desired, serve with sour cream or salsa.

Eggplant Parmesan

PREP TIME: 20 minutes
COOK TIME: 35 minutes
TOTAL TIME: 55 minutes
YIELD: 4 servings

(Eggplant is a high-fiber, low-calorie food that is rich in nutrients and offers a multitude of health benefits. It can reduce the risk of heart disease, help with blood sugar levels, and assist in weight loss. It is also extremely versatile and easy to add to any diet.)

INGREDIENTS

1 tablespoon olive oil

2 eggs, beaten

¾ cup seasoned bread crumbs

Salt and pepper, to taste

1 medium or large eggplant, sliced

1 (24-ounce) jar marinara sauce

¾ pound fresh mozzarella, sliced

INSTRUCTIONS

1. Preheat the oven to 450°F. Brush a 9×13-inch rimmed sheet pan with 1 tablespoon olive oil.
2. Heat the sheet pan in the oven for 10 minutes.
3. In a medium shallow dish, beat the eggs. Place the bread crumbs in a second medium dish. Add salt and pepper to taste.
4. Dip each eggplant slice in the egg, then in the bread crumbs.
5. Remove the sheet pan from the oven.
6. Place the eggplant slices on the sheet pan in a single layer. Bake for 8–10 minutes, or until the undersides are crisp and browned. Flip the slices over, and continue baking 8–10 minutes, or until the other sides are also crisp and browned.
7. Top the eggplant with marinara sauce and mozzarella. Return the pan to the oven and bake for another 10–15 minutes, until the cheese is melted. Rotate the pan halfway through baking time.

Sweet Citrus Salmon

PREP TIME: 10 minutes
COOK TIME: 10–12 minutes
TOTAL TIME: 20–22 minutes
YIELD: 4 servings

Salmon is rich in omega-3 fatty acids, which have a lot of heart-related benefits. It is also a great source of lean protein and potassium. Many would argue that it is one of the world's healthiest foods. In fact, the American Heart Association recommends eating at least two 3½-ounce servings of fatty fish like salmon every week.

INGREDIENTS

¼ cup orange juice

3 cloves garlic, minced

3 tablespoons honey

1 teaspoon freshly grated ginger

2 tablespoons soy sauce

1 bunch asparagus, trimmed

1 tablespoon olive oil

Salt and pepper, to taste

1 orange, sliced

4 (6-ounce) salmon fillets

INSTRUCTIONS

1. Preheat the oven to 400°F. Line a 13×18-inch rimmed sheet pan with parchment paper or coat with nonstick cooking spray.
2. In a small sauté pan over medium-high heat, bring the orange juice to a boil. Allow to reduce to half the quantity, about 2 minutes. Add the garlic and cook until fragrant. Add the honey, ginger, and soy sauce and allow to cook until the sauce thickens enough to coat the back of a spoon.
3. Lay the asparagus on the sheet pan and toss lightly with olive oil, salt, and pepper. Top with orange slices.
4. Place the salmon fillets on the sheet pan next to the asparagus. Pat dry with a towel, and season with salt and pepper. Brush half of the glaze on the salmon.
5. Bake for 10–12 minutes or until salmon flakes easily with a fork.
6. Brush the salmon with the remaining glaze.

Tofu and Vegetables

PREP TIME: 10 minutes
COOK TIME: 35 minutes
TOTAL TIME: 45 minutes
YIELD: 4 servings

(Curry powder adds a powerful punch to this simple and very filling meal. As an alternative to curry powder, you can use an equal amount of coriander and cumin.)

INGREDIENTS

16 ounces extra-firm tofu, cut into ½-inch cubes

¼ cup olive oil, divided

1 teaspoon curry powder

Salt and pepper, to taste

1 large bulb fennel, cored and cut into wedges

1 pint cherry tomatoes, halved

1 bunch asparagus, trimmed

INSTRUCTIONS

1. Preheat the oven to 400°F. Line a rimmed 13×18-inch sheet pan with parchment paper or coat with nonstick cooking spray.
2. Spread tofu cubes on a paper towel. Cover with a second paper towel and press to remove as much moisture as possible.
3. In a small bowl, combine 3 tablespoons olive oil, curry powder, salt, and pepper to taste. Add tofu and toss to coat.
4. Spread tofu on the sheet pan in a single layer. Add fennel, taking care not to overcrowd the pan. Roast 20 minutes.
5. Add tomatoes and asparagus to the sheet pan. Drizzle with remaining olive oil and season with salt and pepper.
6. Roast an additional 15 minutes, until tomatoes are very soft and asparagus is tender.

Shrimp "Boil"

PREP TIME: 10 minutes
COOK TIME: 20 minutes
TOTAL TIME: 30 minutes
YIELD: 4 servings

(Shrimp is high in several vitamins and minerals and is a rich source of proten without much fat. Eating shrimp may promote heart and brain health due to the levels of omega-3 fatty acids.)

INGREDIENTS

4 ears corn on the cob, husk on

1 pound baby red potatoes

1 tablespoon olive oil, divided

1 tablespoon cajun seasoning, divided

1 pound large raw shrimp, peeled and deveined

1 pound smoked sausage, cut into 1-inch slices

2 lemons, cut into wedges

4 tablespoons butter, melted

INSTRUCTIONS

1. Preheat the oven to 425°F. Line a 13×18-inch rimmed sheet pan with parchment paper or coat with nonstick cooking spray.
2. Microwave the corn cobs on high for 5 minutes. Shuck and then cut into 2-inch slices.
3. Toss the potatoes with 1 tablespoon olive oil and 1 tablespoon cajun seasoning. Transfer to the sheet pan in a single layer.
4. Bake potatoes for 10 minutes.
5. Add the corn, shrimp, sausage, and lemons to the sheet pan.
6. Bake for 10 minutes, or until shrimp is cooked through.
7. Serve with melted butter. Top with fresh squeezed lemon, if desired.

Stuffed Portobello Mushrooms

PREP TIME: 10 minutes
COOK TIME: 20–30 minutes
TOTAL TIME: 30–40 minutes
YIELD: 4 servings

(Something about the flavor of the runny egg and the spinach is one of my favorite things ever. This dish works great for breakfast, lunch, or dinner.)

INGREDIENTS

4 portobello mushroom caps, cleaned, stems removed

1 tablespoon olive oil, divided

Salt and pepper, to taste

3 cloves garlic, minced

6 ounces baby spinach

1 cup cream cheese, softened

4 large egg yolks

½ cup shredded mozzarella cheese

INSTRUCTIONS

1. Preheat the oven to 450°F. Line a rimmed 13×18-inch sheet pan with parchment paper or coat with nonstick cooking spray.
2. Brush the mushroom caps lightly with olive oil and season with salt and pepper. Roast for 15–25 minutes, or until tender. Carefully discard any excess moisture that has collected.
3. In a medium sauté pan, heat remaining olive oil over medium-high heat. Add garlic and stir until fragrant, about 1 minute. Add spinach and stir. Season with salt and pepper. Stir until wilted. Remove from heat.
4. Spoon equal amounts of spinach into each mushroom cap. Then spoon ¼ cup of cream cheese on top of spinach, leaving a well for the egg yolks.
5. Place an egg yolk into each mushroom cap. Top with mozzarella cheese and some black pepper.
6. Bake for about 5 minutes or until the cheese is melted and the egg is just set.

Chipotle-Lime Shrimp

PREP TIME: 10 minutes
COOK TIME: 10 minutes
TOTAL TIME: 20 minutes
YIELD: 4 servings

(I don't know why, but to me shrimp has always felt like a "fancy" food, which makes it perfect for parties. This meal will be sure to wow your friends, and will require very little effort from you!)

INGREDIENTS

¹/₃ cup lime juice

¼ cup butter, melted

1 teaspoon chipotle powder

2 cloves garlic, minced

1 teaspoon cumin

2 tablespoons minced fresh cilantro

Salt, to taste

2 pounds uncooked shrimp, peeled and deveined

3 limes, sliced

INSTRUCTIONS

1. Preheat the oven to 400°F. Line a rimmed 13×18-inch sheet pan with parchment paper or coat with nonstick cooking spray.
2. In a small bowl, combine lime juice, butter, chipotle powder, garlic, cumin, cilantro, and salt to taste.
3. Arrange shrimp on the sheet pan. Pour lime juice mixture over the shrimp. Top with lime slices.
4. Bake until shrimp turn pink, about 10 minutes.

Garlic Butter Shrimp

PREP TIME: 15 minutes
COOK TIME: 8–10 minutes
TOTAL TIME: 23–25 minutes
YIELD: 4 servings

(I like to pair this dish with a light salad and rice to contrast the heaviness of the butter.)

INGREDIENTS

½ cup butter, melted

4 cloves garlic, minced

1 tablespoon lemon juice

½ teaspoon dried Italian seasoning

Salt and pepper, to taste

2 lemons, sliced

1½ pounds medium shrimp, peeled and deveined

2 tablespoons chopped fresh parsley

INSTRUCTIONS

1. Preheat the oven to 400°F. Line a rimmed 13×18-inch sheet pan with parchment paper or coat with nonstick cooking spray.
2. In a small bowl, combine butter, garlic, lemon juice, Italian seasoning, salt, and pepper.
3. Lay slices of lemon in a single layer on the sheet pan.
4. Place shrimp on the sheet pan in a single layer on top of the lemon slices. Drizzle butter mixture over the shrimp and gently toss to combine.
5. Bake for 8–10 minutes or until shrimp is pink, firm, and cooked through.

Asian Salmon

PREP TIME: 5 minutes
COOK TIME: 10–12 minutes
TOTAL TIME: 15–17 minutes
YIELD: 4 servings

(This salmon pairs really well with rice or salad. I also recommend a bag of stir-fry vegetables as an easy addition!)

INGREDIENTS

¹/₃ cup soy sauce

2 tablespoons rice vinegar

2 tablespoons sugar

1 tablespoon sesame oil

2 cloves garlic, minced

4 skinless salmon fillets

INSTRUCTIONS

1. Preheat the oven to 400°F. Line a rimmed 13×18-inch sheet pan with parchment paper or coat with nonstick cooking spray.
2. In a small bowl, whisk together the soy sauce, vinegar, sugar, sesame oil, and garlic.
3. Place the salmon on the sheet pan. Brush both sides with the glaze.
4. Bake for 10–12 minutes, or until the salmon flakes easily with a fork.

Sweet Potato Black Bean Sheet Pan

PREP TIME: 15 minutes
COOK TIME: 22–24 minutes
TOTAL TIME: 37–39 minutes
YIELD: 6 servings

(Sweet potatoes are a great source of fiber, vitamins, minerals, and antioxidants. They are great for gut health and also have cancer-fighting properties.)

INGREDIENTS

2 medium sweet potatoes, peeled and diced

2 medium zucchini, sliced

1 (15-ounce) can black beans, drained and rinsed

1 cup corn kernels, canned, frozen, or fresh

3 tablespoons olive oil, divided

3 cloves garlic, minced

Coarse salt and black pepper, to taste

6 large eggs

INSTRUCTIONS

1. Preheat the oven to 425°F. Line a rimmed 13×18-inch sheet pan with parchment paper or coat with nonstick cooking spray.
2. In a large bowl, combine the sweet potatoes, zucchini, black beans, and corn. Add the olive oil, garlic, salt and pepper. Toss to combine. Transfer to sheet pan.
3. Bake for 15 minutes, stirring halfway through, until sweet potatoes are tender.
4. Remove the sheet pan from the oven and create 6 wells. Crack an egg carefully into each well. Season each egg with salt and pepper.
5. Return the sheet pan to the oven and bake for an additional 7–9 minutes or until the eggs are set.

Macaroni and Cheese

PREP TIME: 20 minutes
COOK TIME: 20–25 minutes
TOTAL TIME: 40–45 minutes
YIELD: 8 servings

(Ideally, I like to use multiple kinds of cheese in my macaroni and cheese. But if you are limited in ingredients, the sharp cheddar adds the best bang for your buck, as they say. I also prefer that cheese to be from Vermont, but I am a bit biased.)

INGREDIENTS

1 (10-ounce) package elbow macaroni

5 tablespoons all-purpose flour

Salt and pepper, to taste

1 stick butter, divided

2 cups whole milk

12 ounces sharp cheddar cheese, shredded

1/3 cup bread crumbs

INSTRUCTIONS

1. Preheat the oven to 350°F. Line a rimmed 13×18-inch sheet pan with parchment paper or coat with nonstick cooking spray.
2. In a large pot, boil 6 cups of well-salted water. Add elbow macaroni; stir. Allow to boil for about 8 minutes so that the pasta is slightly less than al dente. Pour into a colander; rinse with cold water.
3. In a small bowl, combine flour, salt, and pepper.
4. In a medium saucepan over medium heat, melt 5 tablespoons of butter. Add flour mixture, and stir with a whisk. Once bubbling, add milk. Continue whisking until the milk thickens; it should coat the back of a wooden spoon.
5. Add 8 ounces of the cheese in handfuls, whisking between additions to allow for the cheese to melt.
6. Once all the cheese has melted, remove the pan from the heat. In a large bowl, combine the elbow macaroni with the cheese sauce. Pour into the sheet pan.
7. Top with the bread crumbs. Slice the remaining butter into thin slices and place on top of the bread crumbs. Top with remaining shredded cheese.
8. Bake for 20–25 minutes, or until the top is golden brown.

Pecan-Crusted Tilapia

PREP TIME: 10 minutes
COOK TIME: 15–18 minutes
TOTAL TIME: 25–28 minutes
YIELD: 4 servings

(I love pecans, but they are expensive and not for everyone. You could really use any nut for this recipe, based on your preference.)

INGREDIENTS

1 cup pecans, crushed

½ cup breadcrumbs

Salt and pepper, to taste

3 tablespoons all-purpose flour

½ teaspoon chili powder

½ cup buttermilk

4 tilapia fillets

INSTRUCTIONS

1. Preheat the oven to 350°F. Line a rimmed 13×18-inch sheet pan with parchment paper or coat with nonstick cooking spray.
2. In a shallow dish or plate, combine the pecans, breadcrumbs, salt, and pepper. In a second shallow dish, combine the flour and chili powder. Pour the buttermilk into a third shallow dish.
3. One at a time, dredge the fillets in the flour, shaking off any excess. Then dip in the buttermilk, allowing the excess to drip into the dish. Finally, dip into the pecan mixture. Transfer to the sheet pan when completed.
4. Bake for 15–18 minutes, or until the fish flakes easily with a fork.

Baked Ratatouille

PREP TIME: 15 minutes
COOK TIME: 60 minutes
TOTAL TIME: 1 hour, 15 minutes
YIELD: 4 servings

Did you know eggplant is a fruit? Typically used as a vegetable in cooking, the eggplant is actually a berry by botanical definition. It has the abilty to absorb flavors into its fruit through cooking so has a lot of versatility in the culinary arts.

INGREDIENTS

1 large eggplant

1 yellow bell pepper, sliced

2 medium tomatoes, cut into wedges

2 medium zucchini, sliced into ½-inch pieces

1 medium onion, thinly sliced

8 cloves garlic, minced

2 tablespoons olive oil

Salt and pepper, to taste

Balsamic vinegar, for drizzling

Optional serving ingredient: pasta

INSTRUCTIONS

1. Preheat the oven to 400°F. Line a rimmed 13×18-inch sheet pan with parchment paper or coat with nonstick cooking spray.
2. In a large bowl, combine vegetables, garlic, olive oil, salt, and pepper. Transfer to the sheet pan in a single layer.
3. Bake for 40 minutes, stirring halfway through. Lower temperature to 300°F, and bake for an additional 10–20 minutes, or until the vegetables are tender and begin to caramelize.
4. Serve drizzled with balsamic vinegar and along with pasta, if desired.

Fish in Brown Butter Sauce

PREP TIME: 15 minutes
COOK TIME: 20–25 minutes
TOTAL TIME: 35–40 minutes
YIELD: 4 servings

(You can substitute your favorite white fish in this recipe if haddock isn't your thing.)

INGREDIENTS

1 pound carrots, cut into 1-inch pieces

1 pound small gold potatoes, halved

2 tablespoons olive oil, divided

Salt and pepper, to taste

4 (6-ounce) haddock fillets

8 tablespoons butter

1 lemon, zested and juiced

3 tablespoons Dijon mustard

INSTRUCTIONS

1. Preheat the oven to 400°F. Line a rimmed 13×18-inch sheet pan with parchment paper or coat with nonstick cooking spray.
2. Toss carrots and potatoes with 1 tablespoon olive oil and salt and pepper. Bake for 10 minutes.
3. Remove sheet pan from oven. Add haddock so that everything is in a single layer.
4. Return the pan to the oven and bake for an additional 10–15 minutes or until the fish flakes easily with a fork.
5. In a small saucepan, melt the butter, stirring occasionally. Once melted, cook until the butter starts to brown on the bottom and it begins to smell slightly nutty. Remove from heat and immediately pour into a small bowl.
6. In the same small bowl, whisk butter together with lemon zest, lemon juice, and Dijon mustard.
7. Either pour sauce over fish once plated, or serve on the side for dipping.

DESSERTS

Cookie Bars

PREP TIME: 10 minutes
COOK TIME: 20 minutes
TOTAL TIME: 30 minutes
YIELD: 12 servings

I made some cookies over the holidays that were a huge hit with my family. Cookies, of course, tend to be a bit of work, and these were especially because they required refrigeration before baking. I decided to turn them into bars to eliminate all of that work, and it worked out beautifully! The dough is very thick, so it may require mixing with your hands in order to integrate the chocolate chips.

INGREDIENTS

1 cup butter, melted

$^2/_3$ cup white sugar

1 cup light brown sugar

2 large eggs, room temperature

2 teaspoons vanilla

3 cups all-purpose flour

1 teaspoon baking soda

1 teaspoon salt

2 cups chocolate chips

INSTRUCTIONS

1. Preheat the oven to 350°F. Line a rimmed 9×13-inch sheet pan with parchment paper or coat with nonstick cooking spray.
2. In a large bowl, cream together the butter and sugars. Add the eggs one at a time, then add vanilla, and beat until combined.
3. In a medium bowl, combine flour, baking soda, and salt. Add slowly to the wet mixture, beating together until combined. The mixture is not very wet, so it should be a fairly solid dough.
4. Fold in the chocolate chips. It is easiest to use your hands for this; the dough is so solid that it is difficult to get the chips to combine with it without some force.
5. Press dough into the sheet pan.
6. Bake for 20 minutes. Dough may seem undercooked, but it will continue cooking once removed from the oven.
7. Allow to cool completely before cutting into squares and serving.

Chocolate Cream Pie with Orange Graham Cracker Crust

PREP TIME: 15 minutes
CHILL TIME: 2 hours
TOTAL TIME: 2 hours, 15 minutes
YIELD: 12 servings

My favorite pie at the holidays was always the chocolate cream pie on the graham cracker crust that my mom made. And while that dessert was always beautiful and delicious as it came, I have tried many variations of it over the years to see if I could make it a little bit better—maybe a little more decadent. I found that making the graham cracker crust myself allowed me to add more flavor than simply modifying the pudding.

INGREDIENTS

1½ cups graham cracker crumbs

½ cup butter, melted

1 tablespoon granulated sugar

1½ teaspoons orange zest

2 (5-ounce) boxes chocolate instant pudding mix

1 can sweetened condensed milk

2 cups milk

Optional serving ingredient: whipped cream

INSTRUCTIONS

1. Preheat the oven to 375°F. Coat a 9×13-inch rimmed sheet pan with nonstick cooking spray.
2. In a medium bowl, combine graham cracker crumbs, butter, sugar, and orange zest.
3. Press crumb mixture firmly into the bottom of the prepared sheet pan.
4. Bake for 6 minutes. Remove from the oven and allow to cool.
5. In a large bowl, whisk together the instant pudding mix, sweetened condensed milk, and milk until smooth. This should start to set while mixing.
6. Pour over the crust and smooth with a spatula, spreading out to the edges of the sheet pan.
7. Cover with plastic wrap, making sure it is touching the top of the pudding.
8. Chill for at least 2 hours before cutting into squares and serving.
9. Serve topped with whipped cream, if desired.

Brownies

PREP TIME: 10 minutes
COOK TIME: 40–45 minutes
TOTAL TIME: 50–55 minutes
YIELD: 12 servings

I really like fudgy, chewy brownies that are a little bit underbaked. Apparently it's popular to like the edges? Not me. Give me all of the fudgy middle pieces. Because of that, I tend to pull my brownies out a little earlier than most. Feel free to leave them in the full 45 minutes or until your desired doneness.

INGREDIENTS

¾ cup butter, melted

¾ cup white sugar

¾ cup light brown sugar

3 eggs, room temperature

¾ cup all-purpose flour

$^1/_3$ cup + 2 tablespoons cocoa powder

½ teaspoon salt

INSTRUCTIONS

1. Preheat the oven to 350°F. Line a 9×13-inch rimmed sheet pan with parchment paper or coat with nonstick cooking spray.
2. In a medium bowl, combine the butter and sugars until creamy with a hand mixer on medium speed. Add the eggs, one at a time, beating until well combined. Slowly add the flour, cocoa, and salt until smooth.
3. Pour the batter into the prepared baking pan.
4. Bake for 40–45 minutes or until a toothpick inserted in the middle comes out clean.
5. Allow to cool completely before cutting into squares and serving.

Lemon Lime Cheesecake

PREP TIME: 20 minutes

COOK TIME: 40–45 minutes

TOTAL TIME: 3 hours, including cooling time

YIELD: 16 servings

(I adore this Lemon Lime Cheesecake. When I first saw the idea it seemed a bit odd, but once I tried it, I was in love! It's perfectly sweet and tart.)

INGREDIENTS

1½ cups graham cracker crumbs

½ cup butter, melted

½ cup + 2 tablespoons sugar, divided

2 (8-ounce) packages cream cheese, room temperature

½ tablespoon lemon zest

2 tablespoons lemon juice

Zest and juice from 1 lime

1 teaspoon vanilla extract

2 eggs + 1 egg yolk

INSTRUCTIONS

1. Preheat the oven to 350°F. Coat a 9×13-inch rimmed sheet pan with nonstick cooking spray.
2. In a medium bowl, combine graham cracker crumbs, butter, and 2 tablespoons sugar.
3. Press crumb mixture firmly into the bottom of the prepared sheet pan.
4. In a large bowl, beat the cream cheese and $1/2$ cup sugar with a mixer on medium speed until smooth, about 2 minutes. Add lemon zest and juice, then lime zest and juice, and vanilla, and mix well.
5. Add eggs and yolk one at a time, and beat on low speed until blended. Pour carefully over crust.
6. Bake for 40–45 minutes or until the cake is just set. Transfer to a cooling rack.
7. Allow to cool on the rack for 30 minutes; transfer to the refrigerator and allow to cool for at least 30 minutes before cutting into squares and serving.

No-Bake Chocolate Peanut Butter Bars

PREP TIME: 20 minutes
YIELD: 16 servings

Every year during the holidays, my family makes what we have always called "bon-bons." I have no idea why we call them that; most people refer to them as buckeyes, and they are some variation of peanut butter covered in chocolate. We have always added crispy rice cereal to ours, and I cannot recommend it highly enough. They are a lot of work, so sometimes I make them into bars, which is a lot easier and quicker.

INGREDIENTS

1½ cups crispy rice cereal

6 tablespoons butter, melted

1 cup powdered sugar

1 cup peanut butter

1¾ cups semi-sweet chocolate chips, melted

INSTRUCTIONS

1. Line a 9×13-inch rimmed sheet pan with parchment paper or coat with nonstick cooking spray.
2. In a large bowl, combine rice cereal, butter, powdered sugar, and peanut butter. Press into the bottom of the sheet pan.
3. Spread the melted chocolate over the bars with a spatula.
4. Refrigerate for at least 2 hours or until chocolate hardens. Cut into squares.

Blueberry Lime Pie

PREP TIME: 5 minutes
COOK TIME: 60 minutes
TOTAL TIME: 65 minutes
YIELD: 8 servings

(Full credit for this pie idea comes from my boyfriend. He says he was making a pie one time and didn't have the lemon juice it called for so he subbed lime juice—and I am sure glad he did, because I love this pie!)

INGREDIENTS

4 cups blueberries

¾ cup white sugar

2 tablespoons cornstarch

Zest and juice of 1 lime

Refrigerated pie crust

INSTRUCTIONS

1. Preheat the oven to 400°F. Line a 6½×9½-inch (⅛th sheet pan) rimmed sheet pan with parchment paper or coat with nonstick cooking spray.
2. In a large bowl, combine blueberries, sugar, cornstarch, lime zest, and lime juice. Set aside.
3. Remove one of the dough rounds from the plastic. Lay over the top of the sheet pan. Press it down so that it completely covers the bottom and sides of the sheet pan. Cut off any excess dough. Set this aside to use later as topping.
4. Prick the bottom of the dough a few times with a fork.
5. Pour the blueberry mixture into the prepared pan.
6. Cut the remaining dough (including the other round from your package) into strips. Set them on top of the blueberries in a criss-cross pattern so that you can still see the blueberries underneath. The amount of dough you use is your preference; I found I used about ¾ of the remaining dough, and that ultimately didn't overpower the flavor of the fruit.
7. Bake for 10 minutes. Reduce oven temperature to 350°F and bake for an additional 45–50 minutes. Blueberry filling should be bubbling.
8. Allow to cool for at least an hour.

Peach Raspberry Pie

PREP TIME: 10 minutes
COOK TIME: 45 minutes
TOTAL TIME: 55 minutes
YIELD: 12 servings

Fun fact about me: I generally don't consider it dessert unless there's chocolate involved. This pie, however, has made me reconsider that stance. It is so incredibly good, you will find it hard not to eat it all in one sitting. It also makes for an amazing summer dessert. In the winter, if you're having trouble finding good fresh fruit, use frozen and increase the cooking time by 15 minutes.

INGREDIENTS

1 round refrigerated pie dough

3 medium peaches, pitted and sliced

2 cups raspberries

1 cup white sugar

3 tablespoons cornstarch

½ cup all-purpose flour

½ cup light brown sugar

5 tablespoons butter, melted

INSTRUCTIONS

1. Preheat the oven to 450°F. Line a 6½×9½-inch (1/8th sheet pan) rimmed sheet pan with parchment paper or coat with nonstick cooking spray.
2. Remove one of the dough rounds from the plastic. Lay over the top of the sheet pan. Press it down so that it completely covers the bottom and sides of the sheet pan. Cut off any excess dough. Prick the bottom of the dough with a fork.
3. Bake dough for 5 minutes. Remove from the oven.
4. In a large bowl combine peaches, raspberries, white sugar, and cornstarch. Set aside.
5. In a medium bowl, combine flour, brown sugar, and melted butter.
6. Pour the fruit mixture into the prepared dough. Top with the crumble mixture by sprinkling over the fruit with your hands. It should nearly cover the fruit.
7. Bake the pie for 10 minutes at 450°F, then reduce the oven temperature to 375°F and bake for an additional 35 minutes.
8. Allow to cool for at least 10 minutes before serving.

Pineapple Upside Down Cake

PREP TIME: 20 minutes
COOK TIME: 45 minutes
TOTAL TIME: 1 hour, 5 minutes
YIELD: 10 servings

(This is another desssert I wholeheartedly enjoy, despite the fact that it is not chocolate. It is incredibly moist and delicious.)

INGREDIENTS

1 stick butter, melted

1 cup brown sugar

1 can pineapple slices, drained

1 jar maraschino cherries

1 box yellow cake mix

3 eggs, room temperature

$1/3$ cup butter, melted

¼ cup milk

INSTRUCTIONS

1. Preheat the oven to 350°F. Coat a 9×13-inch rimmed sheet pan with nonstick cooking spray (parchment paper won't really work with the way we set this cake up).
2. Pour the melted butter into the pan. Sprinkle the brown sugar evenly over the butter. Lay the pineapple slices evenly in the pan, and top each with a cherry. Set aside.
3. In a medium bowl, beat together the cake mix, eggs, butter, and milk.
4. Pour into the sheet pan and spread evenly with a spatula.
5. Bake for 45 minutes, or until a toothpick inserted in the center comes out clean.
6. Allow to cool on a rack for at least 30 minutes. Turn over onto a large cutting board or serving platter.

Saltine Holiday Candy

PREP TIME: 5 minutes
COOK TIME: 20 minutes
CHILL TIME: 1 hour
TOTAL TIME: 1 hour, 25 minutes

If you like salty and sweet, this treat is for you! I use the largest sheet pan I have for this since I typically make this to hand out during the holidays. You can easily reduce the number of crackers, butter, and brown sugar to meet a smaller need. But, honestly, why would you do that? Also, you can add anything your heart desires to the top of this once the chocolate is spread out—nuts, candies, sprinkles, anything!

INGREDIENTS

48 saltine crackers
1 cup unsalted butter
1 cup packed light brown sugar
½ teaspoon vanilla extract
20 ounces semi-sweet chocolate chips

INSTRUCTIONS

1. Preheat the oven to 350°F. Coat a 9×13-inch rimmed sheet pan with parchment paper—this is the ideal way to keep the toffee from sticking.
2. Place saltine crackers on the bottom of the pan in a single layer.
3. In a medium saucepan over medium-high heat, combine the butter and brown sugar and bring to a rolling boil while stirring constantly. Once the mixture is boiling, reduce the heat to medium and allow to simmer for 5 minutes, stirring frequently. It should thicken and be the consistency of a caramel sauce. Watch it carefully so that it doesn't burn or boil over.
4. Remove the pan from the heat and allow it to cool for about 30 seconds. Add the vanilla and stir.
5. Pour the mixture over the saltine crackers evenly, spreading with a spatula if necessary.
6. Bake for 5–7 minutes, or until the toffee becomes bubbly.
7. Remove the pan from the oven and let it rest for 3–5 minutes.
8. Sprinkle the chocolate chips evenly over the pan and let them sit for 3 minutes. The chocolate should begin to melt during that time; you should be able to smooth it over the toffee with the spatula.
9. Allow to cool to room temperature for 30 minutes. Transfer to the refrigerator and allow to cool for at least 1 hour.
10. Break into pieces and store in an airtight container in the refrigerator for up to 2 months or at room temperature for 2 weeks.

Conversion Charts

Metric and Imperial Conversions

(These conversions are rounded for convenience)

Ingredient	Cups/ Tablespoons/ Teaspoons	Ounces	Grams/Milliliters
Butter	1 cup/ 16 tablespoons/ 2 sticks	8 ounces	230 grams
Cheese, shredded	1 cup	4 ounces	110 grams
Cream cheese	1 tablespoon	0.5 ounce	14.5 grams
Fruit, dried	1 cup	4 ounces	120 grams
Fruits or veggies, chopped	1 cup	5 to 7 ounces	145 to 200 grams
Fruits or veggies, pureed	1 cup	8.5 ounces	245 grams
Liquids: cream, milk, water, or juice	1 cup	8 fluid ounces	240 milliliters
Salt	1 teaspoon	0.2 ounce	6 grams
Spices: cinnamon, cloves, ginger, or nutmeg (ground)	1 teaspoon	0.2 ounce	5 milliliters
Vanilla extract	1 teaspoon	0.2 ounce	4 grams

Oven Temperatures

Fahrenheit	Celsius	Gas Mark
225°	110°	¼
250°	120°	½
275°	140°	1
300°	150°	2
325°	160°	3
350°	180°	4
375°	190°	5
400°	200°	6
425°	220°	7
450°	230°	8

About the Author

Sarah Jones is a working mother of three children who keep her incredibly busy. She hates doing dishes more than any other chore, so one-sheet-pan meals are her favorite. She loves reading, gardening, cooking, and spending quality time with her family. She's also the author of *Keto Sheet Pan Cookbook*. She currently resides in Keene, New Hampshire.

Index

A

almonds
    Blueberry Cinnamon Granola, 9
appetizers
    Bacon-Wrapped Dates with Goat
      Cheese, 18
    Bacon-Wrapped Sweet Potato Bites with
      Cheese Dip, 25
    Baked Biscuits with Cheesy Spinach
      Garlic Dip, 20
    Baked Brie, 19
    Chicken Wings with Raspberry Glaze,
      16
    Crispy Baked Ravioli, 23
    Hasselback Baguette, 17
    Loaded Waffle Fries, 27
    Sheet Pan Nachos, 24
    White Pizza Sticks, 21
Apple Crumble, 2
apples
    Pork Tenderloin with Fingerling
      Potatoes, Apples, and Green Beans, 63
arugula
    BLT Pizza with Roasted Garlic Aioli, 61
Asian Salmon, 91
asparagus
    Sweet Citrus Salmon, 82
    Teriyaki Chicken, 36
    Tofu and Vegetables, 83

B

bacon

Bacon, Zucchini, and Goat Cheese
    Frittata, 13
Bacon-Wrapped Dates with Goat
    Cheese, 18
Bacon-Wrapped Mini Meat Loaves, 57
Bacon-Wrapped Sweet Potato Bites with
    Cheese Dip, 25
BLT Pizza with Roasted Garlic Aioli, 61
Egg, Kale, and Bacon Hash, 5
Junk Food Breakfast, 3
Loaded Waffle Fries, 27
Ranch Sheet Pan Burgers and Fries, 68
Bacon, Zucchini, and Goat Cheese
    Frittata, 13
Bacon-Wrapped Dates with Goat Cheese, 18
Bacon-Wrapped Mini Meat Loaves, 57
Bacon-Wrapped Sweet Potato Bites with
    Cheese Dip, 25
Baked Biscuits with Cheesy Spinach
    Garlic Dip, 20
Baked Brie, 19
Baked Ratatouille, 97
Barbecue Chicken Dinner, 31
Barbecue Pork Tenderloin with Green
    Beans and Tomatoes, 49
barbecue sauce
    Barbecue Pork Tenderloin with Green
      Beans and Tomatoes, 49
beans
    black
      Mexican Kale and Beans, 74
      Quesadilla, 79

Sheet Pan Nachos, 24
Sweet Potato Black Bean Sheet Pan, 93
chickpeas
Chickpeas and Vegetables, 75
green
Barbecue Pork Tenderloin with
Green Beans and Tomatoes, 49
Parmesan Garlic Chicken with Green
Beans, 42
Pesto Chicken with Tomatoes and
Green Beans, 45
Pork Tenderloin with Fingerling
Potatoes, Apples, and Green
Beans, 63
beef
ground
Bacon-Wrapped Mini Meat Loaves, 57
Ranch Sheet Pan Burgers and Fries, 68
Sheet Pan Tacos, 60
Stuffed Poblano Peppers, 53
steak
Beef and Broccoli, 71
Philly Cheesesteak, 67
Steak Dinner, 66
Steak Fajitas, 72
Steak Tips, 69
Beef and Broccoli, 71
bell pepper
Baked Ratatouille, 97
Barbecue Chicken Dinner, 31
Chicken Fajitas, 41
Philly Cheesesteak, 67
Steak Fajitas, 72
biscuits
Baked Biscuits with Cheesy Spinach
Garlic Dip, 20
Sausage Gravy Breakfast Pizza, 7

blackberries
Raspberry Blackberry Sheet Pan
Pancakes, 10
blackberry preserves
Baked Brie, 19
BLT Pizza with Roasted Garlic Aioli, 61
blueberries
Blueberry Cinnamon Granola, 9
Blueberry Cinnamon Granola, 9
Blueberry Lime Pie, 106
bread
Hasselback Baguette, 17
Sheet Pan Egg-in-a-Hole, 14
Sheet Pan French Toast, 11
breakfast
Apple Crumble, 2
Bacon, Zucchini, and Goat Cheese
Frittata, 13
Blueberry Cinnamon Granola, 9
Broccoli and Cheddar Slab Quiche, 6
Egg, Kale, and Bacon Hash, 5
Junk Food Breakfast, 3
Raspberry Blackberry Sheet Pan
Pancakes, 10
Sausage Gravy Breakfast Pizza, 7
Sheet Pan Egg-in-a-Hole, 14
Sheet Pan French Toast, 11
broccoli
Beef and Broccoli, 71
Broccoli and Cheddar Slab Quiche, 6
Brownies, 103
Bruschetta Chicken with Balsamic Glaze, 43
Brussels sprouts
Gnocchi and Vegetables, 77

C
cabbage

Kielbasa and Cabbage, 51

cake

Lemon Lime Cheesecake, 104

Pineapple Upside Down Cake, 108

candy

Saltine Holiday Candy, 109

carrots

Chicken Drumsticks and Vegetables, 33

Fish in Brown Butter Sauce, 98

Ham and Pineapple Dinner, 52

cereal

rice

No-Bake Chocolate Peanut Butter
Bars, 105

cheese

American

Bacon-Wrapped Sweet Potato Bites
with Cheese Dip, 25

Brie

Baked Brie, 19

cheddar

Broccoli and Cheddar Slab Quiche, 6

Chili Cheese Pigs in Blankets, 62

Junk Food Breakfast, 3

Loaded Waffle Fries, 27

Macaroni and Cheese, 94

Sausage Gravy Breakfast Pizza, 7

Sheet Pan Egg-in-a-Hole, 14

Stuffed Poblano Peppers, 53

cotija

Mexican Kale and Beans, 74

cream

Baked Biscuits with Cheesy Spinach
Garlic Dip, 20

Lemon Lime Cheesecake, 104

Spinach-Stuffed Chicken, 30

Stuffed Poblano Peppers, 53

Stuffed Portobello Mushrooms, 87

feta

Hasselback Baguette, 17

goat

Bacon, Zucchini, and Goat Cheese
Frittata, 13

Bacon-Wrapped Dates with Goat
Cheese, 18

Egg, Kale, and Bacon Hash, 5

Ranch Kielbasa and Zucchini, 56

gorgonzola

Hasselback Baguette, 17

Mexican blend

Sheet Pan Nachos, 24

Monterey Jack

Quesadilla, 79

Sheet Pan Nachos, 24

mozzarella

Baked Biscuits with Cheesy Spinach
Garlic Dip, 20

Chicken Parmesan, 35

Eggplant Parmesan, 81

Quesadilla, 79

Stuffed Portobello Mushrooms, 87

White Pizza Sticks, 21

Zucchini Sausage Pizza Boats, 55

Parmesan

Crispy Baked Ravioli, 23

Gnocchi and Vegetables, 77

Parmesan Garlic Chicken with Green
Beans, 42

Parmesan Pork Chops, 65

Pesto Chicken with Tomatoes and
Green Beans, 45

Spinach-Stuffed Chicken, 30

White Pizza Sticks, 21

provolone

Philly Cheesesteak, 67
Ranch Sheet Pan Burgers and Fries, 68
ricotta
White Pizza Sticks, 21
Sheet Pan Tacos, 60
Swiss
Chicken Cordon Bleu, 38
cheesecake
Lemon Lime Cheesecake, 104
cherries, maraschino
Pineapple Upside Down Cake, 108
chicken
Barbecue Chicken Dinner, 31
Bruschetta Chicken with Balsamic
Glaze, 43
Honey Mustard Chicken, 37
Parmesan Garlic Chicken with Green
Beans, 42
Pesto Chicken with Tomatoes and
Green Beans, 45
Prosciutto-Wrapped Chicken with Kale
and Potatoes, 39
Spinach-Stuffed Chicken, 30
Teriyaki Chicken, 36
Chicken Cordon Bleu, 38
Chicken Drumsticks and Vegetables, 33
Chicken Fajitas, 41
Chicken Parmesan, 35
Chicken Wings with Raspberry Glaze, 16
Chickpeas and Vegetables, 75
chili
Chili Cheese Pigs in Blankets, 62
Chili Cheese Pigs in Blankets, 62
Chipotle-Lime Shrimp, 88
chocolate chips
Cookie Bars, 100
No-Bake Chocolate Peanut Butter Bars, 105

Saltine Holiday Candy, 109
Chocolate Cream Pie with Orange
Graham Cracker Crust, 101
cocoa
Brownies, 103
Cookie Bars, 100
corn
Barbecue Chicken Dinner, 31
Sheet Pan Nachos, 24
Shrimp "Boil," 85
Sweet Potato Black Bean Sheet Pan, 93
crackers
Saltine Holiday Candy, 109
crescent rolls
Baked Brie, 19
Chili Cheese Pigs in Blankets, 62
Crispy Baked Ravioli, 23

D
dates
Bacon-Wrapped Dates with Goat
Cheese, 18

E
Egg, Kale, and Bacon Hash, 5
eggplant
Baked Ratatouille, 97
Eggplant Parmesan, 81
eggs
Bacon, Zucchini, and Goat Cheese
Frittata, 13
Egg, Kale, and Bacon Hash, 5
Sausage Gravy Breakfast Pizza, 7
Sheet Pan Egg-in-a-Hole, 14
Sheet Pan French Toast, 11
Stuffed Portobello Mushrooms, 87
Sweet Potato Black Bean Sheet Pan, 93

F

fajitas
    Chicken Fajitas, 41
    Steak Fajitas, 72
fennel bulb
    Tofu and Vegetables, 83
Fish in Brown Butter Sauce, 98
french fries
    Junk Food Breakfast, 3
    Loaded Waffle Fries, 27
frittata
    Bacon, Zucchini, and Goat Cheese
        Frittata, 13

G

Garlic Butter Shrimp, 89
Garlic Herb Pork Tenderloin, 59
Gnocchi and Vegetables, 77
granola
    Blueberry Cinnamon Granola, 9
gravy
    Junk Food Breakfast, 3

H

haddock
    Fish in Brown Butter Sauce, 98
ham
    Chicken Cordon Bleu, 38
Ham and Pineapple Dinner, 52
Hangover Savior, 3
Hasselback Baguette, 17
Herby Turkey and Sweet Potatoes, 32
honey
    Sweet Citrus Salmon, 82
Honey Mustard Chicken, 37

J

jalapeño
    Bacon-Wrapped Sweet Potato Bites with
        Cheese Dip, 25
    Steak Fajitas, 72
Junk Food Breakfast, 3

K

kale
    Egg, Kale, and Bacon Hash, 5
    Mexican Kale and Beans, 74
    Prosciutto-Wrapped Chicken with Kale
        and Potatoes, 39
Kielbasa and Cabbage, 51

L

Lemon Lime Cheesecake, 104
lime
    Blueberry Lime Pie, 106
Loaded Waffle Fries, 27

M

Macaroni and Cheese, 94
maple syrup
    Blueberry Cinnamon Granola, 9
marinara sauce
    Chicken Parmesan, 35
    Crispy Baked Ravioli, 23
    Eggplant Parmesan, 81
    Zucchini Sausage Pizza Boats, 55
Mexican Kale and Beans, 74
mushrooms
    Philly Cheesesteak, 67
    Stuffed Portobello Mushrooms, 87
mustard
    Bacon-Wrapped Mini Meat Loaves, 57
    Chicken Cordon Bleu, 38

Fish in Brown Butter Sauce, 98
Honey Mustard Chicken, 37
Steak Tips, 69

N
nachos
Sheet Pan Nachos, 24
No-Bake Chocolate Peanut Butter Bars,
105

O
oats
Apple Crumble, 2
Blueberry Cinnamon Granola, 9

P
pancakes
Raspberry Blackberry Sheet Pan
Pancakes, 10
Parmesan Garlic Chicken with Green
Beans, 42
Parmesan Pork Chops, 65
parsnips
Chickpeas and Vegetables, 75
pasta
Macaroni and Cheese, 94
Pesto Chicken with Tomatoes and
Green Beans, 45
pastry, puff
Broccoli and Cheddar Slab Quiche, 6
Peach Raspberry Pie, 107
peanut butter
No-Bake Chocolate Peanut Butter Bars,
105
Pecan-Crusted Tilapia, 95
pecans
Blueberry Cinnamon Granola, 9

Pesto Chicken with Tomatoes and Green
Beans, 45
Philly Cheesesteak, 67
pie
Blueberry Lime Pie, 106
Chocolate Cream Pie with Orange
Graham Cracker Crust, 101
Peach Raspberry Pie, 107
pineapple
Ham and Pineapple Dinner, 52
Pineapple Upside Down Cake, 108
pizza
BLT Pizza with Roasted Garlic Aioli, 61
Sausage Gravy Breakfast Pizza, 7
White Pizza Sticks, 21
Zucchini Sausage Pizza Boats, 55
poblano peppers
Stuffed Poblano Peppers, 53
pork
Barbecue Pork Tenderloin with Green
Beans and Tomatoes, 49
Garlic Herb Pork Tenderloin, 59
Parmesan Pork Chops, 65
Pork Tenderloin with Fingerling
Potatoes, Apples, and Green Beans, 63
Pork Tenderloin with Fingerling Potatoes,
Apples, and Green Beans, 63
potatoes
Chicken Drumsticks and Vegetables, 33
Egg, Kale, and Bacon Hash, 5
Fish in Brown Butter Sauce, 98
Ham and Pineapple Dinner, 52
Junk Food Breakfast, 3
Pork Tenderloin with Fingerling
Potatoes, Apples, and Green Beans, 63
Prosciutto-Wrapped Chicken with Kale
and Potatoes, 39

Ranch Sheet Pan Burgers and Fries, 68
Shrimp "Boil," 85
Steak Dinner, 66
sweet
    Bacon-Wrapped Sweet Potato Bites
      with Cheese Dip, 25
    Chickpeas and Vegetables, 75
    Herby Turkey and Sweet Potatoes, 32
    Sweet Potato Black Bean Sheet Pan, 93
Prosciutto-Wrapped Chicken with Kale
  and Potatoes, 39
pudding mix
  chocolate
    Chocolate Cream Pie with Orange
      Graham Cracker Crust, 101

Q
Quesadilla, 79

R
ranch dressing
  Loaded Waffle Fries, 27
Ranch Kielbasa and Zucchini, 56
Ranch Sheet Pan Burgers and Fries, 68
raspberries
  Peach Raspberry Pie, 107
Raspberry Blackberry Sheet Pan
  Pancakes, 10
raspberry jam
  Chicken Wings with Raspberry Glaze, 16
ravioli
  Crispy Baked Ravioli, 23
rice
  Beef and Broccoli, 71

S
salmon

Asian Salmon, 91
  Sweet Citrus Salmon, 82
salsa
  Sheet Pan Nachos, 24
Saltine Holiday Candy, 109
sausage
  Kielbasa and Cabbage, 51
  Ranch Kielbasa and Zucchini, 56
  Sausage Gravy Breakfast Pizza, 7
  Sheet Pan Egg-in-a-Hole, 14
  Shrimp "Boil," 85
  Zucchini Sausage Pizza Boats, 55
Sausage Gravy Breakfast Pizza, 7
Sheet Pan Egg-in-a-Hole, 14
Sheet Pan French Toast, 11
Sheet Pan Nachos, 24
Sheet Pan Tacos, 60
shrimp
  Chipotle-Lime Shrimp, 88
  Garlic Butter Shrimp, 89
Shrimp "Boil," 85
spinach
  Baked Biscuits with Cheesy Spinach
    Garlic Dip, 20
  Spinach-Stuffed Chicken, 30
  Stuffed Portobello Mushrooms, 87
Spinach-Stuffed Chicken, 30
Steak Dinner, 66
Steak Fajitas, 72
Steak Tips, 69
Stuffed Poblano Peppers, 53
Stuffed Portobello Mushrooms, 87
Sweet Citrus Salmon, 82
Sweet Potato Black Bean Sheet Pan, 93

T
tacos

Sheet Pan Tacos, 60
Teriyaki Chicken, 36
teriyaki sauce
Beef and Broccoli, 71
tilapia
Pecan-Crusted Tilapia, 95
Tofu and Vegetables, 83
tomatoes
Baked Ratatouille, 97
Barbecue Pork Tenderloin with Green
Beans and Tomatoes, 49
BLT Pizza with Roasted Garlic Aioli, 61
Pesto Chicken with Tomatoes and
Green Beans, 45
Ranch Kielbasa and Zucchini, 56
Tofu and Vegetables, 83
tortilla chips
Sheet Pan Nachos, 24
turkey
Herby Turkey and Sweet Potatoes, 32

V
vinegar
apple cider
Honey Mustard Chicken, 37
balsamic

Bruschetta Chicken with Balsamic
Glaze, 43
Chicken Wings with Raspberry
Glaze, 16
Steak Tips, 69
white
Teriyaki Chicken, 36
white wine
Chicken Cordon Bleu, 38

W
walnuts
Blueberry Cinnamon Granola, 9
White Pizza Sticks, 21
wieners
Chili Cheese Pigs in Blankets, 62

Z
zucchini
Bacon, Zucchini, and Goat Cheese
Frittata, 13
Baked Ratatouille, 97
Ranch Kielbasa and Zucchini, 56
Sweet Potato Black Bean Sheet Pan, 93
Zucchini Sausage Pizza Boats, 55

Also Available

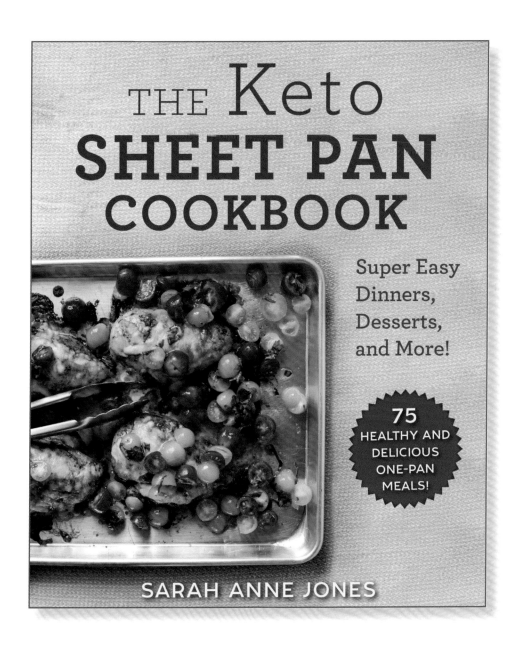

THE *Keto* SHEET PAN COOKBOOK

Super Easy Dinners, Desserts, and More!

75 HEALTHY AND DELICIOUS ONE-PAN MEALS!

SARAH ANNE JONES

Notes

Notes

....

....

....

....

....

....

....

....

....

....

....

....

....

....

....

....

....

Notes

....

....

....

....

....

....

....

....

....

....

....

....

....

....

....

....

....

Notes

....

....

....

....

....

....

....

....

....

....

....

....

....

....

....

....

....

....

Notes

Notes

Notes

....

....

....

....

....

....

....

....

....

....

....

....

....

....

....

....

....

....

Notes